Taunton's DECKS COMPLETE

EXPERT ADVICE FROM START TO FINISH

The Taunton Press

The Taunton Press, Inc.,
63 South Main Street, PO Box 5506,
Newtown, CT 06470-5506
e-mail: tp@taunton.com

Editor: Peter Chapman
Copy editor: Candace B. Levy
Indexer: Jim Curtis
Jacket/Cover design: Kimberly Adis
Interior design: Kimberly Adis
Layout: Cathy Cassidy
Illustrator: Mario Ferro
Photographer: John Ross, except where noted

Library of Congress Cataloging-in-Publication Data
Grice, Scott.
  Decks complete / Scott Grice and John Ross.
      pages cm
  Includes index.
  ISBN 978-1-62113-011-6
1. Decks (Architecture, Domestic) I. Ross, John, 1969- II. Title.
  TH4970.G755 2015
  690'.893--dc23
                              2014046453

Printed in the United States of America
10 9 8 7 6 5 4 3 2 1

Construction is inherently dangerous. Using hand or power tools improperly or ignoring safety practices can lead to permanent injury or even death. Don't try to perform operations you learn about here (or elsewhere) unless you're certain they are safe for you. If something about an operation doesn't feel right, don't do it. Look for another way. We want you to enjoy working on your home, so please keep safety foremost in your mind.

Writing, like all crafts, is a shared endeavor. There is my co-author, John Ross, who provided both the impetus and overall drive for this book. There is Peter Chapman, who calmly shepherded our words from scribblings on note cards to the text you now hold in your hands. Behind John and Peter stand armies of book folks—copy editors, graphic designers, illustrators, photo editors, and so on. Many I will never know or meet, but I'm indebted to them all for making this book a reality.

And then, of course, there is my family—Annabeth, Io, Layla, and Harper—who make it all matter.

contents

>> >> >> >>

INSTALLING RAILINGS
162

DECK STAIRS
190

DECK MAINTENANCE
208

INTRODUCTION

A DECK IS THE PERFECT MARRIAGE of America's best-loved household spaces: the kitchen, the living room, and the yard. It's a place where the entire family can cook, eat, entertain, and socialize all in one space. In the summertime, it is the modern equivalent of the hearth room of the family homestead. With about 2 million decks built or replaced each year, it is arguably the most common home upgrade—and with good reason. Building a deck is an approachable project that adds value to a home and improves the experience of living in it. The materials are readily available. The necessary tools and know-how are easily within reach of the average homeowner, and you will get more bang for your buck per square foot building a deck than any other home improvement project.

Why We Build Decks

Decks, as an architectural feature of houses, are a relatively modern phenomenon. Before World War II few houses included a deck, but now almost all new houses are built with one. Houses have always offered the opportunity to spend time outdoors: You could go out on the porch or patio or maybe the veranda; and many older homes had exterior balconies or maybe even a gazebo. But why the sudden and rapid growth in the popularity of decks?

To answer this question, we need to look at how the planning and building of houses changed after World War II. Housing boomed after the war. Before, and during the war, economic necessities forced extended families to live together under one roof. Once the war was over and the American economy started to expand, the rising economic tide meant that Americans had money to spend. What Americans wanted to buy was a home, a single-family residence. To meet this demand, builders reinvented the way houses were built. After 1945, houses became mass-produced products. Efficiency in building materials and techniques was required at every juncture. This change in construction went hand in glove with the Modernist spirit that dominated architecture at the time. Architects, especially west of the Rockies, were designing simple, modular houses with informal transitions among the living spaces inside the house and an easy flow from inside to outside.

Rear-facing exterior walls now contained a lot of glass, and concrete patios extended the living space out into the yard. But as the boom continued and buildable lots became scarcer, more hillsides were developed. This change in topography presented challenges for using concrete to extend the interior of the house. The extra work required to build patios on sloped sites made these structures cost prohibitive. Porches were a possibility but their roof structures were hard to incorporate with the Modernist style. Balconies offered no means of access to the yard. Decks were seen as a solution. Easily modified to accommodate any topography, with a minimalist aesthetic that matched the Modernist spirit of the time, decks became the architectural feature of choice to extend the usable living space into the exterior environment.

The Role of Wood Preservative

Porches do a good job of protecting what's underneath, but it didn't take a rocket scientist to figure out that an unprotected deck will rot. In fact, for as long as wood has been used in construction, attempts have been made to protect wood from decay. Oils, tar, pitch, and arsenic have all been used as wood preservatives. In the 19th century, creosote oil was the main preservative used for railroad ties and telegraph poles. Creosote protects wood from decay well but has several drawbacks, including its smell and the fact that the oil seeps back out from the wood. For railroad ties and utility poles, these drawbacks are minimal but, within the setting of someone's home, these drawbacks become a deal breaker.

Other forms of wood preservation had been developed during the Industrial Revolution, mainly using pressure to force chemical preservatives deep into the interior of the wood. Pressure-treated lumber had industrial applications but gained its foothold in residential construction by way of deck building. Pressure-treated lumber didn't smell, nor was it oily to the touch. It was durable and affordable. As it gained a greater presence in our homes, concerns grew about the chemicals used to treat the wood. The industry responded by removing arsenic from the slew of preservatives used to treat the wood. These changes have not lessened the public's desire for "cleaner" forms of preserved wood. The industry continues to research alternatives, and today there are promising nonchemical alternatives of baked or pickled products.

The Challenge of a Well-Built Deck

Decks are unprotected structures. Not only do they have to withstand UV radiation and seismic forces but they also have to resist the damaging effects of biodegradation, freeze-thaw cycles, insects, acts of God, acts of children, and many other maladies. They also have to be aesthetically inviting places where someone wants to spend time. Decks also have to work. Decks are tools, masquerading as spaces. If the deck doesn't work, if it is not big enough to accommodate the family, or if it

restricts the flow between house and yard, it won't get used as it should. It may be beautiful to look at and be made to last for ages, but if it's not useful then it won't have much value. Building decks, like building most structures, comes down to three broad questions: What

A DECK BUILDER WEARS MANY HATS

A person who builds decks is, among other things, part designer, part laborer, part project manager, and part client. Not only will you need to wear all these hats at different times but you'll also need to switch among them. There is clarity in the chaos, though. If you take the time to draw out a detailed plan and work schedule before you begin, you'll get used to wearing many hats at once.

is the deck's function? What will the deck look like? What is the best way to build it? We will spend some time discussing functionality and aesthetics (see "Designing a Deck," p. 6), but most of this book is dedicated to how to build decks.

How This Book Can Help

Like any how-to manual, this book provides detailed instructions on how to build a deck from design to finish. More than that, though, we hope this book provides some insight into how to think like a deck builder. How is this different from knowing the instructions for building a deck? There is no way a book can cover all the possible scenarios encountered by deck builders working across North America and beyond. But a good deck builder can walk onto any construction site and build a good deck, regardless of site conditions, aesthetic demands, or code requirements. How does this happen?

Best deck practices

- Don't build for now, build for 20 years down the road. You're not building for the newborn, but for the 20-year-old who will inevitably host an outdoor dance party on the deck you're building.
- Don't skimp. If you think it's expensive to build a deck the right way, try cutting corners. You'll find it's not a wise or inexpensive option.
- Plan ahead. When the actual building of the deck begins, there should be no more wondering about whether the deck will be 12 ft. wide or 11 ft. wide.
- Be present while you work. About 98% of accidents come from not paying attention.
- Measure once, cut once. But be right about your measurement.
- Know the difference between *structurally sound* and *aesthetically pleasing*. All framing must be the former but rarely has to be the latter.
- Craftsmanship is environmentally friendly.
- Remodeling is more difficult than new construction.

Experience is a large part of the answer, and though a book can never replace experience, it can inform that experience by stressing ways to think and practices to adopt that are essential to any good deck builder. There is one practice that anyone thinking about building a deck should begin now: Start looking at decks and try to evaluate them. Start with decks you like and decks you don't like. Ask your neighbors if they like their decks and if they would do something differently if they could. Then ask yourself if you agree with them. Sharpening the eye does two things. For the homeowner looking to build a deck, this process will help you gain perspective and give you some fresh ideas. For the person looking to become a deck builder, determining your likes and dislikes will help with designing decks for other people.

A deck builder is a jack-of-all-trades. You will need to think like a designer, an excavator, a framer, a finish carpenter, and, of course, a client. Building a deck also means that you will exert a lot of control over what the deck will look like and how it will be built. Even if you are planning to hire subcontractors for portions of the job, this book can help you understand the whole process and anticipate problems. Whenever possible in this book, we strive to give you options to adopt for your own project. What is absolutely crucial in a coastal environment may be overkill in the desert. Reading this book will help guide you through the process of designing, planning, and building a deck of your own.

DESIGNING A DECK

THERE ARE TWO DISTINCT PHASES TO the design process. The creative phase is the first phase and the most fun. This is the time when everyone gets to put on his or her dreaming cap and ask, What sort of deck could we build here? For the creative phase, budgets are unlimited, logistics are of no concern, and the weather will always be perfect. Out of the creative phase your dream deck will emerge.

Next comes the adaptive phase, which is still satisfying because it is in this phase that the idea of the dream deck can, with some reasonable modifications, turn into a realistic plan. In the adaptive phase, your ideas are modified to reflect the realities of code requirements, budget limitations, and property boundaries. While the creative phase is the fun part, the adaptive phase can be more of a challenge; the more you explore both of these aspects of design, the better your deck will fit your specific needs.

DESIGNING A DECK THAT WORKS FOR YOU

Creating Usable Spaces, p. 8

ORIENTING YOUR DECK

Relationship between House and Yard, p. 16

STRUCTURAL DESIGN

Design from the Top Down, p. 18

Your Deck and the Code, p. 24

CREATING USABLE SPACES

Regardless of how beautiful a deck is, if we can't use it, it will frustrate us. Form does follow function, so when envisioning your dream deck, first think of what you want the deck for: entertaining, relaxing, grilling, hot-tubbing, sunbathing, or some combination of all these activities. Get all possible uses down on paper and play with ideas. As you organize your thoughts, you'll soon discover which uses are central to you and which are peripheral. This is the creative phase. Enjoy it!

Once you have an idea of how you want to use your new deck, then you can play with size and shapes that both appeal to your aesthetics and accommodate your uses. One way is to simply stand in the space in your yard and imagine what you'll be doing. Maybe you want to look at the view while you're grilling. Conversely, maybe the view is not so great so you want the focus to be around a central seating area. Or maybe you just bought your dream home and all you want to do is sit outside and look back at the house. Whatever you plan to do, the direction of the primary focus will influence the size and shape of your deck.

After you've spent some time in the space, you'll want to get your ideas down on paper. This will help you track and organize the different options. The best way to draw the deck is as if you were looking down on it, known as a plan view. There are deck-design programs that can help with this (see "Deck Design Software Can Be Helpful" on the facing page), but an easy way to do the same thing is to make an interactive drawing. Simply put, an interactive drawing is an outline of the deck shape with scaled pieces of paper cut to the size of different features you want to include (see "Use a Deck Drawing to Avoid Common Errors" on p. 10). While this type of drawing is not as fancy as computer software, it does have the distinct advantage of a simple user interface.

This space was clearly designed for the view. It's large enough to allow people to walk comfortably around the chairs but is not too big. The railing system enhances the view rather than detracts from it.

The designer of this deck made a smart move by creating a dining area large enough to avoid feeling cramped (foreground) and a smaller area for sitting and enjoying the forest view.

This space is too small for a breakfast table. Getting in and out of the chairs will undoubtedly mark up the siding. A bench might work better in this space.

DECK DESIGN SOFTWARE CAN BE HELPFUL

The benefit of deck design software is that it creates 3D renderings of your deck so you can really see what things will look like.

There are many software options out there. Some cost money, others are available online for free. A decking professional who needs to generate 3D renderings for clients should plan to buy software for the extra features and reliability. For everyone else, it makes more sense to choose one of the free online deck design tools.

Most of the online programs start with a generic design that you then modify to simulate the deck you want to build. Depending on your ability and the usability of the program, this experience can raise your blood pressure a hundred points.

Some of the online programs–Big Hammer (www.bighammer.com), Lowe's® (www.lowes.com), and Home Depot® (www.homedepot.com), for example–have a free-form deck option that makes it easier to represent your deck, but there is still a bit of a learning curve. A nice feature of the Lowe's Deck Designer program is that it will generate a price for the deck you design, along with a materials list. Remember that what such a program specifies may not be code approved in your municipality.

One option is to do an initial design with pencil and paper. With that in hand, you can go to the local lumber store and have one of the techies enter the specs into the software. He or she can then generate a rendering. After any modifications are made, the store's program can easily generate a materials list and then a price. Customer service is worth something.

CREATING USABLE SPACES (CONTINUED)

While this deck is elegant and well made, **it would not be usable for someone who has trouble navigating stairs. However, as a bridge from the living space of the house to the yard below, it functions very well.**

USE A DECK DRAWING TO AVOID COMMON ERRORS

A drawing like the one shown at right (albeit using drafting software) is what architects use to plan a deck and will help you avoid the most common error in deck design: making a deck that is too small.

If you're not sure how much room you need, mark it out in real space then transfer that back to a drawing. Doing this allows you to see how a 3-ft.-wide table actually needs close to 9 ft. of clearance. If the space around the table is too tight, people will bang their chairs against the railing as they scoot out or they will have to squeeze by to get around someone who remains seated. Either way it's a recipe for frustrated diners.

DRAW OUT THE FUTURE DECK

Make a plan of your deck to locate the areas of key usage.

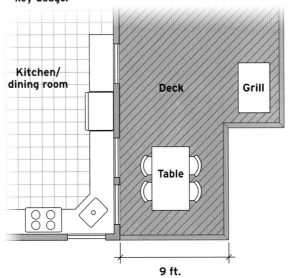

Kitchen/dining room

Deck

Grill

Table

9 ft.

Grade-level decks

Decks that are at or within a step of the ground are called grade-level decks. Grade-level decks provide a good transition between the home's interior and the landscaped grade. They are also an inexpensive way to cover a concrete patio poured in a moment of aesthetic amnesia by the previous homeowner. Grade-level decks do present some special challenges during construction, like extra excavation, cramped working spaces, and moisture management since the frame of the deck restricts air flow underneath. However these challenges are often offset by the advantages of an overall simplicity in the framing design and no need for a handrail or stairs.

This grade-level deck helps protect the landscaping by providing a walkway while also enhancing the house's architectural look.

If possible, grade-level deck boards should be gapped **farther apart** and air vents should be installed in the rim of the deck. These additions will increase airflow and help prevent rot and mildew.

CREATING USABLE SPACES (CONTINUED)

Elevated decks

Why settle for good when you can make it great? This is the idea germ that has replaced countless living room windows with sliding-glass doors opening to a deck that was not there before. Remember the dream phase of deck planning we discussed a few pages ago? Well now is the time to soak it up. Go and enjoy that great view out your window and imagine your dream deck just outside. If you have the view, a well-crafted deck can make you feel as though you were stepping out into the sky. The pinch, of course, is that elevated decks are expensive and difficult to build, but don't think about that now. Stay focused on the dream.

➜ For a reality check see "Engineering an Elevated Deck" on the facing page.

The details of this elevated cantilevered deck **required that the framing be tied back into the main structure of the house. During construction, custom scaffolding was erected because the grade drop-off was too steep for a crane or standard scaffolding.**

Above the treetops. **One of the most attractive advantages of an elevated deck is that it allows you to get above it all. This elevated deck was framed as a cantilever.**

Framing for an elevated deck does not have to be complicated. This deck at the main-floor level has simple post-and-beam framing. Hanging baskets act as a screen to the storage area below.

ENGINEERING AN ELEVATED DECK

The higher a deck is off the ground, the greater the engineering and safety modifications required to build it. An elevated deck may not be as high as you think. Depending on the local jurisdiction, a deck only 30 in. above grade will require modifications to protect the deck users as well as the structure. The higher the deck rises above grade, the more protection is required, and this protection, especially for the integrity of the structure, will increase in both complexity and cost the higher the deck gets.

FIRST LEVEL
Anything above 30 in. up to around 8 ft. is considered a first-level deck. Generally, a secure, code-compliant attachment to the house along with typical cross bracing will be sufficient. However, in areas prone to high wind or seismic loads, even a first-level deck design may need to be approved by an architect or engineer.

SECOND LEVEL
Second-level decks are 8 ft. to 20 ft. high. The construction of these decks is more complex because of increased dead and live loads, increased wind loads, and vertical distribution of seismic loads, which increase as height and weight increase.

THIRD LEVEL
The cost and complication of any deck above 20 ft. will increase significantly. If you just have to have the view and there's no other way to obtain it, be prepared to pay and to have some patience.

Note: A fall from any height can result in serious injury. Always protect both those working up high as well as anyone who might pass below.

COST AND COMPLICATIONS RISE WITH THE DECK

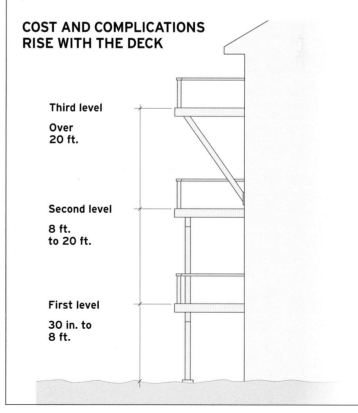

Third level

Over 20 ft.

Second level

8 ft. to 20 ft.

First level

30 in. to 8 ft.

CREATING USABLE SPACES (CONTINUED)

Creating curves

Curves have an innate appeal, perhaps because of the way they soften a boundary or add visual interest to an otherwise ordinary setting. Even something as simple as a curved handrail can be inviting to the eye and touch. Or it could be that curves in the built environment are somewhat rare and are therefore something special. Building a curved deck from dimensional lumber is difficult. However, where natural materials struggle, synthetic decking can shine.

Many types of synthetic decking have significant natural flexibility. Some can even be heated in special steamers, allowing radical bends in decking to create unique patterns.

Rooftop decks

There are times when the area that would be perfect for a deck is already taken by another part of the house. If the view you want is best seen while standing on the addition you put in 5 years ago, then a rooftop deck is definitely an option worth exploring. This is essentially an elevated deck that borrows its support from another structure. A rooftop deck has the advantages of a better view and improved privacy without the disadvantage of having to build the involved framing needed for an elevated deck. That said, you still have to build it on a roof, which is not that easy and will require permits, an engineer's approval, and possibly a roofing contractor experienced in this type of project.

Curves are difficult to incorporate into a deck. The math used to lay out a curve can be complicated and a lot of room may be needed to transfer the curve onto the physical space. Curves are not for the faint of heart but can add an elegant appeal to a deck that is hard to create in other ways.

Sometimes there is no place to put a deck other than on the roof. This deck grants the homeowners a spectacular view of the ocean over their neighbors' rooftops.

Rooftop decks require extra planning. This deck over a garage carries the extra load of large planter boxes for the homeowner's kitchen garden. While the structure can carry the weight and there is no leakage below, no one anticipated the mildew from the soil that is growing on the fascia where the runoff flows.

Decks that carry extra loads

Decking, framing, and people are assumed loads when designing a deck. Something really heavy like a hot tub, large planter boxes, or machinery needs to be accounted for with extra engineering. The higher the deck, the more expensive and complicated the project. Of course, decks can be built to carry nearly any load that a residential setting would require but, as with elevated decks, be prepared to pay.

Wraparound decks

Creating a deck around a pool has several advantages over a concrete pool surround. First, wood looks better than concrete and it feels better to walk on and lay on. The disadvantages are the potential for rot and a surface that gets slippery when wet or with mildew buildup. Wise material choices will minimize the threat of rot. The slip factor can be controlled by the material itself. Some materials come with ridges in the surface, which breaks the surface cohesion and thus the slip factor. There are also aftermarket products that can be applied to the wood to achieve the same result by creating traction, but as you can imagine these will also add to the abrasiveness of the surface.

Multilevel decks

Some living spaces don't work well when built on more than one plane. The sunken living room, for example, was a fad that allowed us to discover that navigating three steps with a tray of Buffalo wings and a jug of beer is a hazard we may not want to introduce into our home simply for the sake of architectural intrigue. A multilevel deck, however, is another story. Decks on different levels not only provide visual interest but also help you use the deck better by creating different areas of focus. Multiple decks can also be pieced together with patios and paths to create living spaces with different textures for different uses.

A separate structure with bigger posts and more bracing was built to carry the load of the hot tub rather than trying to incorporate all the design needs into a single deck. However, given the deck's age and the updated seismic requirements in this location, it's doubtful that this deck would pass code if built today.

This small wraparound deck not only provides a comfortable place to sit at the edge of the hot tub but also conceals the plumbing.

Multiple levels can help define outdoor rooms where walls don't do the job. On this deck, the sunken area is clearly a place designed to encourage you to slow down and enjoy the view.

RELATIONSHIP BETWEEN HOUSE AND YARD

Typically, the more permanent aspects of your home—such as the position of the back door or where the lot line is located—establish the deck location. Orienting your deck is a much different story. As touched on previously, you'll want to decide on the focus of the deck to help establish how you'll shape and use it.

There are times when a deck is simply an extension of the house and the yard isn't part of the equation. Conversely, a deck may belong more to the yard than it does to the house. In other situations, a deck acts as a bridge from the house to the yard. Whatever the case, to use the space efficiently, take extra time to draw out the traffic patterns. Once the patterns are established you can make adjustments to ensure you use the space efficiently.

Sun, rain, privacy

It stands to reason that if you sit outside without the protection of solid walls and a roof, you will be more exposed to the elements and to your neighbors. Decks are designed for both public and private consumption and will be designed very differently depending on how public the deck will be. For example, height relative to the surroundings adds to the privacy. More privacy can be gained by adding screens, arbors, or pergolas. Also, simple boundaries that don't block the vision but still help define the space can add a sense of privacy. Decorative railings, flowering trees, or evergreen bushes can all help establish visual and physical boundaries.

As with privacy, protection from the elements does not have to be complete. Often, if a small section of a deck is protected from the sun or rain it will be enough of a haven. If you do have the opportunity to cover part of the deck, consider designing the space for a bench or a pair of chairs so you can wait out the rain shower in comfort.

Maybe more than any other feature, railings can define the look and feel of a deck, whether they be classic or, like here, ultra modern.

Shading can be a simple screen, or you can go big with a pergola that shades the entire deck. Pergolas add quiet and a sense of privacy.

This deck was designed for the opposite of privacy, or so it seems. The deck is on the front of the house, low to the ground and without a buffer to the street, like a railing or screen. While this makes the deck more public than a traditional front porch, it also creates a streetside focal point, adding to the privacy of the living room. The large deciduous tree increases the privacy while providing welcome shade.

Incorporating a bench into the railing helps unite the yard below with the raised deck. During gatherings, people sitting on the bench can feel part of the action of both the deck and the yard.

This garage-top deck was exposed to the street, but adding a thick planter around the perimeter blocked both noise and prying eyes, effectively creating a private retreat within feet of passing cars.

DESIGN FROM THE TOP DOWN

By this point, we hope you've had fun dreaming and have a pretty good idea of what you want or at least what you want to use your deck for. Dreaming up a deck is usually exciting, and the next part of the design process—of actually hammering out a design that works—can be enjoyable as well. However, fewer people find it so. You can hire a designer or an architect to take over the structural design, but if the deck is modest, there's no reason not to tackle the design on your own.

It's too much to cover everything about structural design here; that's a different type of book. Instead, you'll gain an understanding of the structural parts of a deck and how they work together. Even if you have experience building a deck, the following sections will be valuable in updating or confirming your understanding of how a deck works.

Given that the structural requirements of a deck trump aesthetic concerns and that most loads the deck has to resist come from the top down, we typically start designing from the top of the deck down. Usually this means starting with the railings and the decking, the two elements most driven by aesthetic concerns. This approach still pays off given all the code requirements for how the railing posts tie into the deck's frame and how different decking patterns will require special joist layouts.

Railings

Typically, railings are already included in the dead-load value given for decks, so they require no special attention in that regard. But railings are prone to significant lateral loads that require specific construction methods too.

Gone are the days when the railing posts were simply lag-bolted to the rim joist. New code requirements put more emphasis on creating a connection that can resist a concentrated live load applied in any direction (see "Securing Newel Posts" at right).

➡ See "Installing the Newel Posts," p. 168.

Deck railings are a system of components, **anchored by posts, that keep you, your family, and guests safely topside.**

SECURING NEWEL POSTS

Securing the newel is not as simple as connecting it to the rim with bolts. The rim must also be secured to the joist to resist the lateral load transferred from the newel. The minimum size for wood railing posts is 4×4 because the post must be able to resist bending under the applied force.

In addition, any part of the infill of the railing system (anything below the guard rail) has to be able to resist a 50-lb. force per square foot area. Most conventional infill systems meet this requirement, but it is good to remember if a custom system is to be used.

Always consult your local building department for specific requirements where you live.

Drawing adapted from the *Prescriptive Residential Wood Deck Construction Guide* (DCA-6; American Wood Council, 2013)

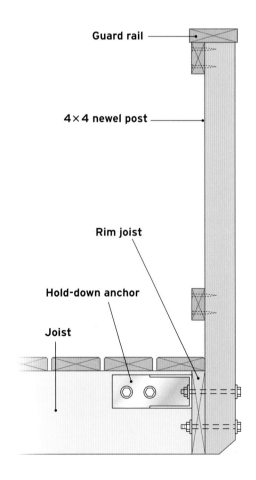

Guard rail
4×4 newel post
Rim joist
Hold-down anchor
Joist

Decking

Different types of decking material may require different framing details. Most standard wood decking requires 16-in. on-center (o.c.) spacing for the joists. With some thicker dimensions, the spacing can be increased to 24 in. o.c. Some types of synthetic decking don't have the rigidity of natural wood and so require joist spacing at 14 in. or even 12 in. o.c. It is always important to follow the manufacturer's recommended guidelines. Any sort of concentrated load that rests on decking should have appropriately sized framing directly underneath the load to ensure proper transfer.

Joists

Joists are almost always 2× dimensional lumber. The job of the joist is to direct the diffuse loads of the deck and concentrate it to the beams. Because the ledger is usually in plane with the joists, hangers are used to transfer the load on the joists to the ledger. At the other end, joists typically sit on top of a beam. If the beam is in plane with the joists, then hangers are used there too. Most often the beam is below the line of the joists. This has the advantage of allowing the joists to extend beyond the beam (cantilever). This cantilever helps hide the beam from view. To help the joist assembly stay upright, the space between the joists is blocked over the beam and the ends are attached to a rim joist.

Joists support the deck (left) but need help. Once the joists are fitted and secured, blocking is added to create a solid assembly (right).

MAKING THE JOIST ASSEMBLY SOLID

Since the joist assembly as a whole adds stability to the entire deck, it's important to make secure connections.

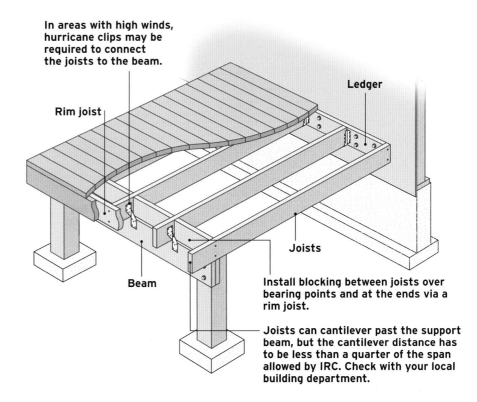

In areas with high winds, hurricane clips may be required to connect the joists to the beam.

Rim joist

Ledger

Joists

Beam

Install blocking between joists over bearing points and at the ends via a rim joist.

Joists can cantilever past the support beam, but the cantilever distance has to be less than a quarter of the span allowed by IRC. Check with your local building department.

TRADE SECRET

For help on deciding what lumber to use for framing and how to use it, visit the American Wood Council website (www.AWC.org). There you'll find everything from span tables to prescriptive building guides with detailed construction notes.

DESIGN FROM THE TOP DOWN (CONTINUED)

Ledgers

Most decks attach to the house on one side by means of a ledger. The ledger is essentially a joist that runs perpendicular to the field joists of the deck (and parallel to the rim joist on the outside of the house frame). All the field joists transfer their load to the ledger by means of hangers. The ledger transfers these loads to the foundation of the house by means of bolts or lags. The details will differ, depending on the construction details of the house.

➡ See "Installing Ledgers," p. 91.

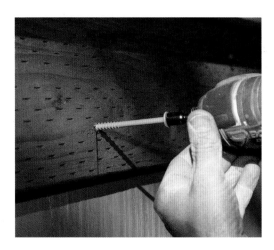

Ledger attachment **requires some knowledge of the house's framing details to ensure the ledger will be properly secured.**

Five common pitfalls of ledger attachment

■ The ledger-to-house attachment must be visible for inspection. If the connection to the house's floor system or the load path within the house cannot be verified, the deck may well need to be independently supported. Ledgers are attached to the house with lag bolts or through bolts. Code requires that lag bolts project 1/2 in. beyond the rim joist of the house's floor frame so the inspector can verify that the bolts are the proper dimensions. The framing members of the house also need to be inspected to ensure they are capable of handling the load of the deck.

■ Ledgers cannot be attached to brick veneer.

■ Ledgers cannot be attached to fireplaces or chimneys.

■ Ledgers cannot be attached to cantilevered sections of the house. Code allows connections to the house only where the structure of the house has support below.

■ When lag bolts or through bolts are used to connect the ledger to the house, the following pattern is required: They must be placed 2 in. from the bottom or top of the ledger and 2 in. to 5 in. from the ends of the ledger. Fasteners must be staggered from top to bottom along the horizontal run of the ledger.

WHY NOT JUST SKIP THE LEDGER?

As crazy as it may sound, if you want to build a grade-level deck adjacent to a house with a crawl space, skipping the ledger might be the best option. Given all the detailing that goes into the ledger board, including flashing and waterproofing as well as verifying the load path to the inspector, it may well be easier to make the deck freestanding.

Here are some details to consider. If your permit requires that the inspector verify bolts and shear anchors, a freestanding deck has a lot of advantages: no siding work, no waterproofing the ledger board–house interface, no lingering worries that water is infiltrating the home's envelope, and no invasive demo work.

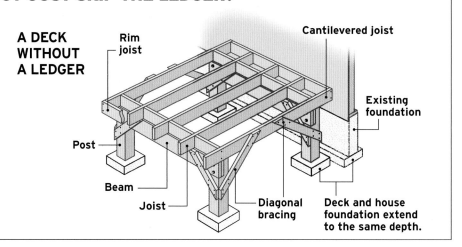

A DECK WITHOUT A LEDGER

Rim joist

Cantilevered joist

Post

Beam

Joist

Diagonal bracing

Existing foundation

Deck and house foundation extend to the same depth.

Posts

If you look through the International Residential Code® (IRC), the "Prescriptive Residential Wood Deck Construction Guide" (DCA-6), or most deck construction guides (see Resources on p. 216), you will have difficulty finding information about how to properly size your deck posts. Span tables for beams and joists are readily available but not load tables for wood columns. One reason is that posts have to support a load straight down but are also subject to lateral deformation, and this changes with the height of the post. That means that the taller the post, the easier it is for it to buckle under a compressive load. This complex relationship between load and post height makes for a gray area. Some guides will recommend that all posts be 6×6. However, for a simple deck only a few feet off the ground, this might be overkill. By using the table below, you should be able to find the right post for your situation. If you are unsure, opt for the more substantial option. And always remember to check with your local building department.

Posts are usually 4×4 or 6×6, **depending on your construction details.**

SELECTING POST SIZES

Follow the chart as a guide to help you decide what size posts to use. Be sure to check with your local building department, and if at all in doubt, opt for the larger post size.

Consideration	Use 6×6 Posts	Use 4×4 Posts
Post height	>8 ft.	<4 ft.
Diagonal bracing	Not needed (for post integrity) up to 14 ft.	Recommended for over 4 ft. high
Loads	High seismic or wind loads	Low seismic and wind loads
Frequency	Fewer posts	Many posts

DESIGN FROM THE TOP DOWN (CONTINUED)

Beams

Like joists, beams concentrate the load above. The joist span will determine the maximum beam spacing, but the site details will figure in as well. On a typical deck that is supported on one end by a ledger and on the other by a beam, the distance of the beam from the ledger is determined by the span capabilities of the joist used. Joist span affects the beam used because the longer the joist span, the larger the area of deck the beam will have to support and thus the beefier it will need to be.

The size of the beam used—anything from a 4-in. by 6-in. wood beam up to an 8-in. by 14-in. GLULAM® beam—is determined by the span of the joists and the number of posts used to support the beam. There are some additional considerations that may also affect this decision. If windows look out beneath the deck, then a big support beam below the joist may noticeably limit the view. If this is the case, consider connecting the joist to the beam with hangers, allowing you to raise the beam to align it to the joist tops. If too many posts interfere with the view, you can reduce the number by increasing the beam size for longer allowable spans. Finally, the beam size will determine the post size because the post will need to be equal to or greater than beam width.

Hardware

The important thing to remember is that all hardware used in deck construction needs to meet a threshold of corrosion resistance. Pressure-treated lumber contains a lot of copper. The copper acts as both fungicide and insecticide. But copper also corrodes steel.

Corrosion happens sometimes when two dissimilar metals come in contact with each other. A small electrical current will begin to flow between the two metals. This current will accelerate the corrosion of the metal that is most reactive. Copper is more stable than steel, so when the two come in contact the steel suffers corrosion. Water (especially saltwater) acts as a catalyst in this process, speeding up the corrosion of the steel. The ways to combat this corrosion are to use hardware made out of stainless steel or copper. The most common way to limit corrosion is to use hardware galvanized with zinc.

➤ See "Framing hardware and fasteners," on p. 58.

The only coating that will adequately protect the steel is a factory-applied hot-dipped galvanized coating. This coating is applied to the steel by dipping the steel in a vat of molten zinc. While the fastener is in the vat the iron in the steel reacts with the zinc, creating a bonded coating. The zinc doesn't protect the steel in and of itself. Rather the zinc undergoes oxidation in the environment. Once the zinc has oxidized, it creates a very stable, nonreactive coating. As long as this coating is thick enough, the hardware will survive for the life of the deck.

During construction, framing elements can be temporarily secured with screws or nails.

These pieces of decking hardware have been dipped in vats of molten zinc to provide a galvanized coating that will help protect them against corrosion.

To save time during assembly, the post-to-beam connections can be installed after all the framing is in place.

Deck foundations don't have to be elaborate, **but they do need to be located precisely and installed properly to prevent disruption by frost heave.**

Setbacks and property boundaries

In addition to all the other codes associated with building, there are also codes that restrict where structures can be built on your property. These restrictions are called *setbacks*, which are basically buffer zones in which nothing can be built. The size and restrictiveness of these setbacks differ from district to district, but almost all municipalities have them. Their primary function is to prevent the spread of fire from one structure to another. They also ensure that one house will not be so imposing as to block sunlight or the flow of air to its neighbors.

Foundations

The first step in designing a foundation is to contact the local building department. You'll want to find out how deep to extend the foundation, how large the foundation needs to be for the soil at your site, and what other considerations you will have to account for. Reviewing your ideas with the building department will determine if a permit is even needed to build your deck. In some locales if a deck is low enough to the ground, a permit is not needed. If you think you won't need a building permit for your deck, it is still a good idea to review your project with your local building department because setback and lot coverage restrictions may still apply.

Decks typically have pier foundations—individual bearing points rather than a continuous foundation, which most houses have. These deck piers will also be referred to as footings. Technically, a footing and a pier are different, but in a practical sense they are almost interchangeable. There are two essential conditions that will determine the size and shape of your footings.

First, you'll want to find out the bearing capacity of the soil. This is the amount of weight per square foot your soil can support. There are two ways to determine the bearing capacity of the soil. The first is to call your local building department and find out the default bearing capacity for the soil in your area. The other is to hire a soils engineer to test your soil. Most people choose the first option because most decks aren't that heavy and the footings aren't that big,

even if the bearing capacity of the soil is low. As decks get bigger and more complex, however, it makes more sense to get the soil tested.

Second, you'll want to determine the tributary load of the deck. This will tell you how much weight you are putting on the footings; combine this with the bearing capacity and you can easily figure out how big your footing needs to be. Determining the tributary load for the whole deck is a straightforward affair and will be covered in "Footings and Foundations" on p. 66.

See "Calculating Footing Size," p. 70.

DESIGN FROM THE TOP DOWN (CONTINUED)

Stairs

It seems that there are more code restrictions surrounding the construction of stairs than almost any other feature of a deck. Surprisingly, though, the structural requirements stipulated by code are somewhat thin. Mostly code provides broad parameters of what loads stairs must carry and leaves it at that. Like the rest of the deck, stairs have to be able to support a 50-lb.-per-square-foot load uniformly distributed across the entire stairway. For example, a stairway that is 36 in. wide and has five treads, each measuring 12 in., has a total square footage of 15 sq. ft., which means that the stairway will have to resist 750 lb. of load. The stairs will create a concentrated load where they tie into the deck frame. Make sure to account for this added weight in your joists, beam, post, and footing calculations. The load will also be used to size the grade beam (a short rectangular concrete foundation) at the bottom of the stairs.

The other structural requirement is that the treads must be able to resist a concentrated load of 300 lb. over a 4-sq.-in. area. For some decking materials this will mean installing extra stair stringers to support the decking.

➡ See "Deck Stairs," p. 190.

Inspectors are notoriously nit-picky when it comes to stairs, so be sure to take extra care with the stair design and construction.

YOUR DECK AND THE CODE

If a permit is required, the building department will provide information detailing what documents you need for the application. Every jurisdiction will have slightly different requirements, but all will require that a set of building plans be submitted with the application. These plans will be reviewed to ensure that the proposed deck complies with all applicable building codes.

Most building departments use the IRC as at least a general framework for the codes adopted within that jurisdiction. The IRC provides minimum standards for a whole range of issues, ranging from safety to energy conservation. The building code is not a how-to of building. It does not (and cannot) provide instructions on how to build a deck on to the back of your house because every house would end up having a designated code for just that one location. Rather, the code defines minimum standards that all structures must meet if they are to be approved—that is, recognized as a legal structure by the governing municipality. Some of these standards can easily be incorporated into any design: 4-in. baluster spacing, for instance. Others, like the appropriate size of a footing, require detailing a continuous load path and indicating how the footing will resist that load.

The DCA-6, mentioned earlier, provides prescriptive deck construction methods that meet or exceed the minimum requirements of the IRC. Because much of what happens in deck building is considered alternative (not specifically detailed in the IRC), the DCA-6 is a great reference tool. In fact, if you build a deck that looks like the one in the DCA-6, then the document itself will most likely provide proof that your deck meets code requirements.

Like stairs, deck railings have numerous code requirements, from height and baluster spacing to attachment and lateral-load details.

Of course, this assumes your local building department recognizes the DCA-6.

Your local building department may supply prescriptive details on the size and shape of acceptable footings. However, it will be the responsibility of the designer to make those details site specific. Often the prescriptive details will not be applicable to a particular location. When an alternative design is employed, most building departments will require approval from a licensed engineer. If you are designing your own deck, you should probably count on getting an engineer's stamp for your plans, unless the deck will be close to ground level without any concentrated loads, such as a hot tub. This doesn't mean that an engineer needs to design your deck; rather, the engineer simply needs to review your work and sign off on it.

Decks are load-bearing structures. Understanding how decks resist the loads imposed on them is critical for understanding why decks are built the way they are.

In many areas, **decks less than 16 in. above grade don't require a railing system, which can create an appealing deck-yard transition.**

Terminology for types of deck loads

- **DEAD LOAD** The weight of the building material itself. To save the trouble of having to add up all the components of the deck to figure out the overall weight of the deck, most building departments accept the default weight of 10 lb. per square foot. So a 100-sq.-ft. deck will have a dead load of 1,000 lb. Typically this estimate is raised to 20 lb. per square foot if tile or a concrete product is used for the decking.

- **LIVE LOAD** The weight of all the people and moveable objects that could be on the deck. The default estimate is 40 lb. per square foot.

- **UNIFORM LOAD** Both the live load and dead load. All the beam-span tables and joist-span tables assume uniform loading of live and dead loads.

- **TRIBUTARY LOAD** The weight of all uniform, live, and dead loads of the deck supported by an individual component of the deck structure.

- **CONCENTRATED LOAD** The weight of a single heavy object. A hot tub is a good example of a concentrated load. Without special support, concentrated loads will exceed the bearing capacity of the structure below. Consequently, the standard span tables should not be

employed if your deck will have concentrated loads.

- **LATERAL LOAD** A force directed horizontally toward the deck. Examples of lateral loads are wind, earthquakes, and people. The lateral loads of wind and seismic activity vary greatly from region to region, so check with your local building department to see what is required. Some prescriptive building practices are meant to resist the lateral forces generated by activities such as an impromptu dance party. Remember, if you anticipate special features or uses of your deck, consult a licensed engineer.

PLANNING AND PREPARATION

A GOOD WAY TO THINK ABOUT the planning and preparation phase is to consider it as building a bridge between all the design work you have already done and the actual construction and assembly you need to do. Building a stable bridge allows the work to continue smoothly. Build a rickety bridge, on the other hand, and you risk falling into the mire. In designing the deck, you've already tackled much of the tough work of preparation and planning. Now is the time to do the legwork that makes the actual building easier. This legwork includes doing a site assessment, contacting the local building department, brushing up your tool skills, and seriously considering what steps you'll take to ensure your own safety and the safety of others.

CONSIDERING THE TERRAIN

Chances are that you've already visited the project site more than once before the planning stage. You may even live there. However, up to this point the focus has been on envisioning the end product. It's worth visiting the site again with a fresh eye toward feasibility. Some aspects of feasibility are site access, staging, utilities, and safety.

Many decks are designed to take advantage of a good view, but this often means the deck is elevated to some degree. A deck that is only a few feet off the ground isn't considered elevated in terms of construction difficulty, but when the deck is higher than 5 ft. (basically when ladders are necessary for layout and framing), the work will slow down considerably.

The higher the deck, the greater the degree of difficulty when building. For example, lifting beams into place, rolling joists, and even "thinking work" like squaring up the deck all become more difficult because that work needs to happen on a ladder. Fortunately, the more time you spend working off ladders and scaffolding, the more comfortable you will become with it. On the first day or so of working on an elevated structure you might see very little progress. After you begin to learn what your limits are and how to increase efficiencies, the pace will begin to pick up. Don't get too comfortable, however. Never put yourself in a position where you feel unsafe and always take the time to ensure your own safety and the safety of those working with you. Equipment rental outlets are a good resource for acquiring everything from extensive scaffolding to safety harnesses and ropes.

A sloped site adds further complication. Depending on the slope of the grade, everything from walking to setting up a ladder or even cutting materials can be difficult or even downright dangerous. For sloped sites, you might choose to stage and cut materials at the nearest flat spot (like the driveway) and then carry materials to the site. Another way to deal with a slope is to use the deck's framing posts to support temporary plat-

The challenges of site access, staging, safety, and engineering cannot be fully gauged (and accounted for in the cost estimate) without a thorough site assessment. The site assessment for this job involved a walk around the house to determine just how difficult it would be to build an elevated deck on the steep site.

forms that you can work off of while erecting the deck framing and then take down after the deck is built.

The slope, as well as lot layout and landscaping, can affect the access to your site. During the planning stage, you'll want to carefully locate the staging areas and determine whether you can have the materials delivered right to where you will be working or if you should have them dropped in the driveway. Also consider how hard it will be

for you to carry materials or push a wheelbarrow from the drop zone to the work site.

Working more than a few feet off the ground or on a slope will add time to the schedule, cost to the budget, and complicate the logistics. Be sure to leave yourself enough of a cushion. For example, it would be foolhardy to expect to finish the deck on July 3 for a July 4 party. Be kind to yourself: Either begin the project sooner or move the party date.

Managing your project

It's beyond the scope of this book to dive deeply into project management, but if you are new to this kind of endeavor, you will do yourself a favor to at least become familiar with some of the key aspects of organizing a job. Before you begin is the time to create a workflow plan and to revisit some of the bigger logistical problems. During this phase you will need to finalize the budget, write a schedule, submit plans to the building department, and order materials.

■ **FINALIZE THE BUDGET** Specify all the materials to be used in your project. All the decisions about which screws to use or what finish to apply have to be made and priced so the real cost of the deck can be determined.

■ **WRITE A SCHEDULE** Accurately estimating how much time it will take to build something is difficult, especially when you're not sure what you will find when you peel back the siding of an 80-year-old house. If you've never estimated a work schedule before, the general rule of thumb is to develop a schedule by thinking through each phase of the project, with an emphasis on being honest in your estimations of how long it will take, and then add 20% to your estimate.

■ **SUBMIT PLANS** Most building departments require that plans be submitted with your permit application. Depending on the complexity of the deck, most departments will approve your application on the same day. In case they won't or in case your application is incomplete, it's best to apply for your permit early in the process. Having the project delayed because your permit is delayed is a special form of agony.

■ **ORDER MATERIALS** Ask your suppliers about the availability of the materials for your deck. If there is any doubt, go ahead and order the materials. See if your supplier can store the materials for you, if you are not quite ready to receive them. In the worst-case scenario, you'll have to store them at your house for a couple of weeks. Just get some tarps and cover everything up.

   Better this inconvenience than hearing that the decking you want is back ordered and won't be available for 6 weeks.

On this project, a site assessment allowed the author to determine that an existing steel structure could provide the support for a new deck. The new deck, while elevated on a slope, was built almost entirely using only a 6-ft. stepladder.

UTILITY COMPANIES AND THE BUILDING DEPARTMENT

It is important to locate all the utilities beneath the ground where you are working. In addition, it is also good to know where the shut-off valves are for things like water and gas. You might be tempted to skip this step as an unnecessary hassle for a slim chance of hitting a utility when you dig. However, when it comes to existing utilities, there is not much predictability and finding a utility by mistake can be exciting to say the least. There is nothing like the thrill of planting a post-hole digger in the ground and getting sprayed in the face with water, and then frantically running around trying to find the water shut-off valve. In this scenario, the upside is that you hit only a water line and not an electrical wire.

Before construction begins determine what utilities run into and out of your house and where those utilities are located. Your local utility department should have a free utility location hotline, or you can dial 811 anywhere in the country to have your call routed to your local center. Once you contact the utilities, representatives will come out and mark out the supply lines from the street to your house.

Sometimes there are underground surprises, even if you've checked with the local utilities and the lines have been traced ahead of time. If the property has a septic or irrigation system, you may have to check with the local building department for the construction drawings that were submitted with the permits. In any case, it's always best to dig lightly and to be sure to know where those shut-off valves are.

Hose bibs and electrical outlets are only some of the fixtures on the outside of a house that may need to be moved for a deck project. Locate these items well ahead of time, and if you don't feel comfortable moving them yourself, hire a local contractor to do the work. Similarly, projects that involve lighting or hot tubs will require electricians and plumbers, respectively.

Hiring a contractor will add to the budget, but getting approval for and moving utilities shouldn't increase the time it takes to complete the project, as long as you make arrangements ahead of time.

Depending on your project's details, you may be able to draw a workable plan that satisfies the building department; if the deck design is complicated, you might need the professional advice of an architect or engineer. Even if you need to consult a professional, the better your drawings, the lower your costs.

Even while digging a shallow hole, **it's possible to encounter utility lines. Considering the risk, always call 811 before you dig to discover what is below grade.**

INCONVENIENT UTILITIES

Different types of utilities require different subcontractors. During the site assessment, make a list of the contractors you may need to call to relocate different utility features. Outdoor electrical outlets and breaker panels are best dealt with by an electrician ❶.

Moving an electrical meter will require you to call the local utility ❷. A hose bib can be relocated with some basic plumbing knowledge ❸. Air vents for dryers, furnaces, or exhaust fans may require calling a HVAC specialist ❹.

ⓘ TRADE SECRET

Good contractors know that planning ahead saves time and money down the road. Getting a construction permit and building to code shouldn't increase the time it takes to construct the deck, unless you don't plan for it. Having to stop your project in the middle because you didn't file the right paperwork will slow you down and can be costly.

SAFETY APPAREL

Before beginning any construction project, it's important to set aside time to plan for your safety. You could follow every safety rule in the book and still get seriously injured building a deck; conversely, you could break every safety rule and finish your project unscathed, but why take the chance? The point is that you need to be aware while working on the job, and if you hear a little voice in your head saying that you are doing something unsafe, stop. Take a break and approach the task in a different manner. Nine times out of ten, people who've been injured on a building site will say that right before the accident happened they heard that little voice—so pay attention to it.

Wearing the appropriate safety apparel goes a long way toward preventing injuries. Some decisions about apparel are common sense. Flip-flops, for example, would be a really bad choice for job-site footwear as they provide no protection from any possible danger, such as a dropped beam, a slip of the utility knife, or a misfire of the nail gun; invest in good work shoes. Other things like hearing protection and eye protection are easy to use and safeguard vulnerable parts of the body. Gloves do a great job of protecting your hands from minor cuts and scrapes, and durable jeans are also recommended.

Covering exposed joists is an easy way to create a safe working surface until the decking is installed.

WEARABLE SAFETY GEAR

Wearing the right gear will protect your eyes, ears, lungs, and skin.

Protection for your eyes and ears is a no-brainer.

Durable jeans add a surprising amount of protection to your skin and are preferable to shorts even in hot weather.

Shoes must be comfortable and durable. These lightweight shoes have leather tops for added protection.

Plenty of glove manufacturers offer choices that protect your hands from minor cuts and bruises yet still allow you to operate tools and manipulate small objects like screws.

LADDER SAFETY

When using a ladder, it's important to make sure that it is set up solidly and securely so that when you reach out for something there is no chance that the ladder will give way. With extension ladders, it's a good idea to drive a 16d nail into the wood on either side of the ladder and then bend it over the ladder's flange, which keeps the top of the ladder from moving. Once up off the ground, build platforms to make it safe to move around. If there is an obvious hazard, which might be easy to forget, clearly mark it so that it is impossible to ignore. When climbing ladders with loads, keep the weight centered over your body and always have one hand on the ladder frame.

Clearly flag or mark any hazards to protect yourself and anyone else who may come onto the job site.

FIVE WAYS TO BE SAFER ON A LADDER

1. Stay centered. Placing the ladder close to the required cut allows you to avoid reaching out and becoming unbalanced.

2. Stay two steps from the top. Although this rule is commonly broken, get a taller ladder instead of being tempted to teeter on the top of a stepladder.

3. Extend a ladder 4 ft. above the surface you're climbing to. This way the ladder can provide support as you transition to the platform.

4. Use bent nails to prevent the ladder from sliding to the side. Bend nails around the ladder rail on both sides.

5. Think ahead. Every action has a reaction that could put you in harm's way. Here, the author made sure that the beam's offcut would not drop near the ladder base, which could cause him to fall.

TOOL SAFETY

The circular saw is arguably the most useful tool for deck building and also the most dangerous. In addition to all the obvious ways a tool with a spinning blade can be hazardous, circular saws are also heavy. Dropped from any height, if this saw lands on somebody, that person is going to the hospital. Fortunately, both sidewinders and worm-drive saws (see p. 50) have rafter hooks that allow the tool to be hooked over a framing member when not in use. If your saw does not have a rafter hook designed into it, buy an aftermarket hook and retrofit your saw.

➡ See "Tools and Materials," p. 38.

Working on any job site, but especially a deck site, it is difficult not to drag cords along behind you as you and your tools move from one place to another. This can cause the tool cord and the extension cord to separate, leaving you powerless. Sometimes the movement creates a partial separation between the two cords. In this case, power still flows but dirt or water can work its way into the plugs, causing shorts to occur. To prevent these problems, tie the cords together in a big loop. Now when you pull on the cord, the strain goes on the loop and not on where the cords attach. Making the loop large keeps the protective casing of the cords from cracking. Some carpenters use a length of electrical wire to tie the two ends together. If you are working in the rain, a short length of tire tube fitted over the connection will help keep the water out.

Some tools have nifty safety features built in. Even a simple tool like a post-hole digger can be designed with safety in mind. One of the worst aspects of driving a post-hole digger is that the handles can come together forcefully, smashing your knuckles together and making a tough job worse. Ridgid® makes a post-hole digger that prevents this; the handles are molded in a way that leaves a gap, sparing your knuckles (see the photo on the facing page). Of course, you pay for this safety feature, but it is money well spent. When comparing tools before a purchase, determine if a manufacturer has gone the extra mile to include features that reduce injury.

Many new circular saws come with a rafter hook already attached. Check out the safety features when buying new tools.

Tying a loose knot at an electrical cord connection is the simplest way to keep tools plugged in as you move around the job site.

WITH ANY TOOL COMES SOME RISK

The trick to tool safety is knowing the risk and making adjustments.

The handles of this post-hole digger **are designed to protect your knuckles.**

A right-angle grinder is useful, **but operating it without a guard will put your hands at risk.**

When renting a tool, **ask for a demo if you've never used it. A short tutorial on how the tool works can prevent injury.**

WORKING ALONE

Working alone has some challenges; for example, who holds the other end of the board? But with a little ingenuity, it's not difficult to build even a large deck by yourself. The most important thing is to work safely. Or to put it slightly differently, to work so that you feel in control. For something like rolling joists, this is as simple as creating a ledge to hold the other end of the joist from where you are working. For lifting beams, setting tall posts, or setting ledgers, working alone can get challenging. When faced with a challenge, applying mental muscle rather than brute strength is usually more effective.

⟹ See "Rolling Joists," p. 127.

That said, working alone adds complications. In terms of safety, working alone is not inherently dangerous, but if you do get injured there is no one there to help you. Sometimes working alone is more efficient than having a crew because there is no guarantee that the extra help will always be working. In other situations, working alone can be slower by a large factor. Working off ladders is a good example: Two or three people can work together, forming a chain, to move materials and tools to a raised work site, but one person working alone would spend a lot of time climbing up and down the ladder to do the same thing.

Whether working alone or with a couple of helpers, building a deck is inherently dangerous work. Just ask the emergency room staff. The more in control you are, the safer you can expect to be.

Moving lumber alone

Working alone means that eventually you will be hauling lumber around on your own. Even if you are young and strong, the lumber will quickly make mincemeat of your body if you don't use proper technique. Balance is the key. Always keep your body centered over your feet and keep the lumber centered on your body. This allows you to maximize your core body muscle and avoid the torque that can so quickly cause an injury. The photos on the facing page demonstrate how to lift lumber properly.

Developing techniques like clamping a board in place to act as a third hand and hold the joist will help keep you safe and help you work more efficiently.

1. Get a grip. Wrap your fingers under the lumber and make sure you have a good hold before beginning your lift.

2. Brace one end against an immovable object so the beam does not slide away from you during the lift.

3. Shift yourself to the center of the beam. Support the beam's weight as you move by shifting your grip, hand over hand.

4. With your body centered and your hands on opposing edges, carefully lift the beam.

5. To lift a beam to your shoulder, go back to step 2 and walk the beam up in the air until you can rest the center point against your shoulder.

6. Bend your knees and carefully transfer the beam's full weight to your shoulder.

7. Carry the beam by draping your arm over the top, controlling its pitch and point.

TOOLS AND MATERIALS

BUILDING A DECK IS A RELATIVELY straightforward project. However, as with building a house, there are a variety of tasks to complete, from excavation and formwork to framing and decking installation. Each task requires a particular set of tools and materials to get the job done. The list of items needed for each phase of deck building is not long or exotic, but acquiring a good understanding of them help the project progress smoothly.

Because deck building is a popular basic homebuilding project, you'll find a variety of products in the home stores that profess to make the job easier. Some of these products live up to their billing, like the Kreg® jig deck-fastener system (see p. 156), but unfortunately, many do not. In the following pages, you'll find the tools and materials needed to build most any deck. Not all of the mentioned tools are necessary for every deck. In fact, for most projects, you can achieve great results with just a few essential tools. Beyond the basics, we've highlighted the tools that will truly make the work go faster and your job easier.

ESSENTIAL TOOLS

LAYOUT

FOUNDATIONS

FRAMING

DECKING

THE BASICS

A good circular saw is about as essential as it gets. Fitted with different blades, it can cut metal, masonry, plastic, and cardboard as well as clapboards and thick beam stock. New models are lighter, have better features, and incorporate enhanced ergonomic designs.

Some old-schoolers might say that having the right knowledge is essential but having the right tool is a luxury. That said, there are some tools it would be hard to build without. If you already have the basic hand tools (see "What's in the Bags" at right) and a circular saw, you possess the minimum of what it takes to build a deck. Consider buying any additional tools only if they satisfy one of two conditions. First, ask if the tool will help you build a better deck. For example, a good level is far superior than the judgment of your eye when aligning posts to plumb. So, if you don't have a level, go get one if you want to build a better deck. The second condition is a tool's ability to substantially increase efficiency. If you have only one deck to build, a good hand-held circular saw can make almost every cut you will need. Buying an expensive miter saw for a single deck is not justified. But if you have several decks to build, the time saved over all the decks by setting up a good cut station might well outweigh the saw's hefty price.

WHAT'S IN THE BAGS?

No matter what phase of the project you are in, there are a few tools that you will always want to have on you or within reach. For centuries, carpenters have worn tool bags or tool belts around their waist to keep the tools close at hand. Certainly over the course of the job, and even day to day, you can mix and match the tools you carry to make yourself more efficient and keep the bag weight to a minimum. The bags themselves are important for carrying fasteners and tools, so invest accordingly. If you think carpentry might become more than an occasional hobby, buy the best bags you can afford.

- Hammer
- Drill driver
- Tape measure
- Chalkline
- Utility knife
- Screwdriver
- Speed® Square
- Awl
- Pencil
- Prybar/nail puller
- Chisel

TRADE SECRET

Save money by renting. All of the more expensive tools used to build a deck are usually available at your local equipment rental store. The advantages of rental are that you pay for only what you need, you don't have to maintain the equipment, and you have extra space in your shop. However, price it out carefully. Depending on the circumstances, it can sometimes be cheaper to buy the equipment, especially if the job is going to drag out for a while.

TAPES AND OTHER TOOLS

The bare bones of layout tools. It's nice to have tools to make the job easier, but if you have more time than money, these measuring and marking tools will get you most of the way there. Tools shown are an awl for marking and holding the end of the tape and string line, a chalkline that can double as a string line, a 25-ft. tape measure, and a Speed Square.

Batter boards placed outside the deck-framing area enable you to set and mark string lines for footing locations. You can remove the strings while you dig and then reposition them quickly to check the footing location. You can purchase metal batter boards (shown) or make your own from scrap wood.

A quality laser level is invaluable for accurate layout and pretty much essential if you are working alone. The model shown has a remote control so you won't spend time walking back and forth to adjust the settings.

Deck projects vary in complexity and so will the layout tools you'll need. You might be able to lay out a simple deck with a 25-ft. tape measure, layout string, and a few stakes. As the deck plan increases in complexity, a laser lever that judges distance as well as elevation can be very useful on uneven terrain. (Sometimes these are called laser measurers.) Other items that are useful during layout include a 100-ft. tape measure (and a helper to hold the dumb end of the tape), marking spray, and some lumber to make a batter board.

FOUNDATION TOOLS

The critical tools for foundations are fairly pedestrian: a string line, a post-hole digger, a wheelbarrow, and a hoe or hard rake. These tools will get the job done. If you have many holes to dig or the ground is especially hard, mechanized digging tools can save you some time and prevent a sore back.

A two-person motorized augur will speed the digging process, but remember to check that the machine has an augur large enough for the footings you need to dig. It is also possible to get an augur attachment on a skid loader. If the loader can navigate on the terrain where you are building, this can make quick work of digging foundation holes.

A step up from a skid loader is a small excavator. As long as the terrain is level and even, operating a small excavator is straightforward and does not require a special license. You also may be able to find a skid loader with a backhoe attachment.

You really don't know what you will find. Here, the hard part was supposed to be cutting through the asphalt of an existing patio—that is until the builders found the old riverbed and the rocks it left behind.

Skid loaders make quick work of moving piles of soil and are relatively easy to operate.

A small backhoe will dig circles around a person with a shovel, but there is a fair amount of peripheral damage so it's not ideal if you want to keep the landscaping looking good.

BASIC DIGGING TOOLS

A hatchet for roots. If you choose to carry a rigger's hammer you will always have a hatchet in your tool bag.

A prybar for rocks. A crowbar can substitute for a prybar but won't provide the same amount of leverage.

The spade tip on the prybar can act as a mini-shovel and cut roots too.

Post-hole diggers are the primary tool for removing dirt, not a shovel, which is more for digging ditches than holes.

Make your job easier by sharpening the spades of your digging tools. A grinder fitted with an abrasive blade sharpens this prybar tip with a few passes.

TRADE SECRET

You're not always comparing apples to apples when considering buying or renting. Renting a power chopsaw to cut masonry beats the price of renting a rolling carriage and masonry blade for a circular saw, and the power chopsaw gets the job done three times faster. However, if cutting concrete runs longer than a day, the tables are turned and you're better off buying a masonry rig for your circular saw and having it available whenever you want.

FOUNDATION MATERIALS

Once the excavation is complete, it's time to fill the hole back up again with your footing material. Concrete is a great building material and by far the most common foundation material used in deck construction. It's durable, can be formed to almost any shape, and has great compressive strength. Concrete is often reinforced with rebar or wire mesh to add tensile strength to a footing. You might also need to form material and gravel.

Footing tubes are available at most home stores and are an efficient way to form up deck footing. Here, a wheelbarrow's handles make a convenient cut station.

WORKING WITH CONCRETE

The biggest challenge to concrete is the limited working time you have from when water is added to the mixture until when the concrete starts to harden, or cure. Another limitation of concrete is the working temperature. Unless carefully mixed with additives, concrete cannot be poured when the temperature is below freezing because it will not cure properly. Heat can have the opposite effect and cause the concrete to cure too quickly, which reduces the available working time. Humidity also affects working time, with dryer conditions speeding up the curing process. Fortunately, the most favorable conditions for working concrete are also the most favorable for your body to work in. If possible, pick a lightly cloudy day with a forecast of 60°F and no rain.

There are two primary methods of concrete delivery. One is to order ready-mix concrete delivered in a truck. This can be the more expensive option, but depending where you live, there may be suppliers who specialize in small batches. Sometimes they will cut you a deal if you are flexible about when the concrete can be delivered. Some trucks have a hose attachment that can pump the concrete around to the back of your house. If your deck project has a difficult access and you are not keen on going all-terrain with a wheelbarrow full of wet concrete, a pumper truck might be the ticket. Expect to pay extra for the convenience.

The other delivery method is to buy bags of dry concrete and mix it with water on site in either a small stand mixer or by hand in a wheelbarrow. With good technique, mixing up a bag in a wheelbarrow is just as fast as using a mixer, and there's nothing to rent or set up (see, "Mixing Concrete by Hand" on p. 46). Buying concrete in a bag is typically less expensive than getting ready mix delivered, and bags of dry mix are easier to move around the job site than is wet concrete.

Working with concrete may be a messy job, and it pays to clean your tools after use. A quick rinse with water is usually all it takes. An adjustable-flow hose tip (see the bottom right photo on p. 47) keeps you from having to run back to the house every time you want to turn the water on or off.

If the concrete won't be delivered by a pumper truck, the easiest way to move it around the job is before it's mixed. This project involved a narrow, sloped access that would have been difficult to navigate with a wheelbarrow full of wet concrete. Moving the bags, however, was a piece of cake—and half the price of having the concrete pumped into place.

TRADE SECRET

Wet concrete is surprisingly heavy and unstable in a wheelbarrow. Don't try to be more productive by mixing large batches. Even the act of mixing the concrete can topple an overloaded wheelbarrow. It takes the same time to mix two one-bag batches of concrete as it does to mix two bags in one batch, and mixing a single bag take less effort.

Concrete calculator

Estimating the amount of concrete you will need for the footings is a simple calculation of volume: length times width times height. For circular form tubes, use this formula: 3.14 (pi) times diameter times height. If math is not your strong point or your form is irregular in shape, look for an online calculator at the manufacturer's website, a home-store website, or via a general Internet search.

WORKING WITH CONCRETE (CONTINUED)

MIXING CONCRETE BY HAND

Some people might assume that it's easy to mix concrete: Buy a bag of premix, dump it in a wheelbarrow with some water, and mix it up. Sounds simple, until you get a face full of concrete dust or spend 5 minutes mixing a bag when it should take only 2 minutes. Here's a method that makes light work of what can be a tedious task.

1. Fill the bottom of a standard wheelbarrow with about 1½ in. of water.

2. Set the sack of concrete mix on end in the water.

3. Open the bag by making a T-cut with a utility knife and laying back the flaps.

4. Slowly empty the concrete into the water; avoid dumping the bag as this creates dust.

5. The concrete should look like a small island with water all the way around it.

6. Pull some concrete into the water with a stiff rake, then push it back to the island. Repeat, pulling in a little more each time.

7. Mix the concrete until it's the consistency of stiff cottage cheese.

8. Pour the concrete directly into the hole or shovel it into a form.

Rinse off your tools after use. An adjustable-flow hose tip (above) is a time-saver.

USING MANUFACTURED FORMS

Heavy-duty cardboard tubes come in a variety of diameters and are the go-to footing forms for a lot of deck builders.

Bigfoot Systems® produces the original and best-selling pier footing form. The plastic form fits the end of a standard cardboard tube and is also available as an all-plastic form (as shown).

Square Foot® forms also fit standard cardboard tubes and make it easier to calculate the area of the footing.

Certainly the most readily available concrete form is the earth wall of the hole you dig. However, for a variety of reasons, earth-wall forms are not always ideal. Wet concrete will conform to the wall's irregular shape, and in areas subject to frost heave the rough shape of the concrete will make the foundation prone to lifting and settling with the soil. The irregular shape of the hole also means wasted concrete. Fitting a manufactured form inside the hole will save on concrete, which translates into a time and money savings for you.

The most common type of concrete form is a heavy-duty cardboard tube that comes in a variety of diameters and is available at most home stores. The inside of the tube is lined with a release material so it can be easily stripped away from cured concrete protruding above grade. A plastic foot can be added to the bottom of a cardboard form to increase the footing's load capacity. Several companies offer plastic form extensions. Although features vary slightly among brands (one company makes a rectangular form to make it easier to calculate the volume), the most important feature may be availability at your local home store.

TRADE SECRET

Prevent form collapse. If you need to wait a few days between when you backfill around the form and pouring concrete, protect the form by wrapping it in a plastic garbage bag before setting it in place. This will prevent rain or ground water from soaking the cardboard; a soggy form won't hold the soil back. For extra protection, cover the form top with a garbage-can lid.

NONCONCRETE OPTIONS AND PRECAST PIERS

Most deck builders use a concrete-filled hole as the footing, but other options exist. One interesting system is a pin footing by Diamond Pier®. This system is designed for limited impact on the surrounding landscaping during installation. The pier has a reinforced concrete anchor block with guide holes built into it. Pins are driven through these holes into the ground with a demolition hammer. The size of the pin or pipe is determined by the bearing capacity of the soil. Helical piers can also save a lot of digging, but they are not available in all regions (they require installation by a specialty contractor). The system works well in locations with poor soil quality or a high water table.

Many building stores offer precast concrete deck piers. These piers usually come with a fitted recess in the top of the pier that receives the 4×4 deck post or with a metal saddle that serves the same function. Back when decks were considered play structures that could be built any way possible, these precast piers were a great time-saver. There was no need to dig a hole or mix a bunch of concrete when you could just spread these piers around and start building. Nowadays precast piers don't offer the same convenience because, no matter the depth of the frost line, deck footings have to rest on undisturbed soil, which will require some amount of excavation to get to. These piers must also be sized correctly to support the deck and to resist lateral forces. That's not to say that these piers cannot be used, but if you drag 10 of them off the shelf of your local home store before checking your deck design against local code, you might have to drag them right back to the home store because they won't work for your project.

Setting a foundation doesn't always involve digging a hole and making a mess of the landscaping. Pin footings can be a low-impact alternative to traditional pier footings.

Don't assume that because a material is for sale in the home store that it's a good option for your job. These precast footing blocks accept only a 4×4 post and won't comply to code in areas where the footing base must sit more than a few inches below grade, which it almost always does.

SAWS FOR FRAMING

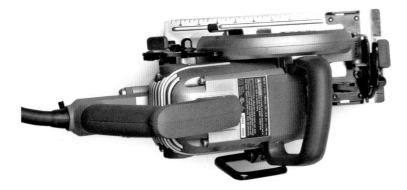

Worm drive or sidewinder? A worm-drive saw (top left) has the motor positioned behind the blade and uses a worm gear to drive the blade. These saws are slightly heavier and more powerful than sidewinders. A sidewinder (bottom left) has the motor positioned to the side of the blade and is often a direct drive.

For depth of cut, nothing beats a circular saw fitted with a Prazi™ chainsaw bar. The main drawback is that the bar has a tendency to wander off line with very deep cuts.

Framing marks the start of the carpentry phase of the project. If you haven't put on your tool bags up to this point, now is the time because almost all the tools in the bags are essential for framing (See "What's in the Bags?," p. 40). In addition to hand tools, you will also need a circular saw. Other tools to consider are levels, drill drivers, and a pneumatic hanger nailer (one brand is Teco®).

> **See "Resources" on p. 216 for company websites.**

It used to be that Skil® and Porter-Cable® brands were the standard-bearers for portable worm-drive or sidewinder saws. However, there are now many brands that make reputable saws in either or both categories including Ridgid, Makita®, DeWALT®, Bosch®, and Milwaukee®.

The question of whether a worm-drive saw or a sidewinder is better is a never-ending debate. Both categories have advantages, and which saw you buy comes down

to personal preference. If you have experience with neither saw, see if you can test some saws before making your purchase because while they may be equal in quality they are definitely different. In this book, the photos show author Scott Grice using a worm-drive saw because, starting as a framer in the western United States, this is the type of saw he learned carpentry with. If you ask a carpenter in the eastern United States what saw he or she works with, most likely it will be a sidewinder.

Beam saws can make a deep depth of cut. A 4× beam is 3½ in. thick, and the typical circular saw can cut only 2½ in. Of course, you can flop the beam over and cut from both sides but that gets tiresome, and for larger beams a 2½-in. cut from both sides still wouldn't be enough. Fortunately, Makita makes a beam-cutting saw with a 16⁵⁄₁₆-in. blade for a maximum cut of 6¼ in. At almost $800, this is certainly a tool you'll want to rent instead of buy. Most equipment rental

stores will carry this saw. A Prazi attachment is also a common beam-cutting option you can rent. This attachment is basically a chainsaw arm that mounts to a standard worm-drive circular saw. The Prazi can be a little less intimidating to operate, but the blade can wander off line if you are not careful with the cut.

Reciprocating saws can be used to finish a beam cut that didn't go all the way through. However, because its blade tends to wander, it's difficult to justify the purchase or rental of a reciprocating saw for a deck project, unless you need to do some demolition beforehand. The finish cut on a beam can easily be made with a good handsaw in about the time it would take to fetch the reciprocating saw from your truck. A multi-tool, on the other hand, has a way of finding itself useful, especially for cutting back siding. If you think you might use it for other projects, a multi-tool is a good investment but certainly not essential.

CUTTING TOOLS FOR DECK BUILDING

Make no mistake, circular saws are important for framing, but building a deck can involve a wide range of tasks and tools. Besides the right-angle grinders and multi-tools already mentioned, here are a few common cutting tools found on deck-building job sites.

A Makita beam saw has a 6¼-in. maximum cut that will get through most beams you'll encounter framing a typical deck.

Circular saws are the workhorse of deck framing and are essential for any deck builder.

Jigsaws let you cut the decking to fit closely around newel posts and door openings.

Chopsaws have their place on a deck project, but be sure to protect them from the elements to keep them working in top form.

LEVELS AND OTHER FRAMING TOOLS

It's key to have a good level on the job. If you can afford only one level, get a 2-ft. level and find a straight 2×4 to set it on when you need to extend the length. A 6-ft. level would be the next to buy because it can span the bows in boards that will cause a smaller level to give an inaccurate reading. Medium-size levels are a luxury and unnecessary if the budget is tight.

A laser level is essential, especially when working alone. It can project a level line over the entire job site that can be used to set the ledger and calculate post heights. A full-featured laser level will run a few hundred dollars, so renting is a good option. There are also simpler laser levels that will self-level but shoot only a single beam. Though not as convenient, these levels are much more affordable.

Two types of pneumatic nailers are also useful for driving the numerous nails required to fasten plate hardware, such as joist hangers. One is a hanger nailer that has a pin (called a positive placement tip) that registers in the hole of the framing hardware. You can save a substantial amount of time when fastening a row of joist hangers, and its easy on your elbow as well. Another type of pneumatic nailer useful for setting hanger nails is a mini impact palm nailer. These nailers act somewhat like the impact wrench a mechanic uses to loosen wheel lug nuts. The nail is held in a sleeve while a mini ram repeatedly strikes the head to drive the nail. As you can imagine, there is some vibration involved, but using one of these is still easier than driving nails by hand.

For other fastening tasks, you can use screws or nails as long as they have the proper galvanic coating. If you plan to use screws, a drill driver is essential, and for nails, a pneumatic nail gun is required. Obviously, for any pneumatic tool you will also need to have hoses and a compressor.

A short level can be made into a long level with a straight board. Here, the author checks the alignment of a run of joists, something he couldn't do using a 3-ft. level by itself.

The luxury of having more than one level comes with a price. Make sure they all read the same and discard or fix the one that is the odd level out. If you don't, you will be chasing your tail to get boards level and plumb every time you pick up a new level.

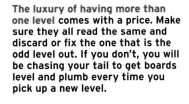

A laser level can project a level line that can be used to set the ledger and calculate post heights.

NAILS VS. SCREWS

The drawback of working with screws is trying to keep the appropriate driver tip handy ❶. Screws are easy to drive, easy to remove, and don't require the driver to be attached to an air hose that has to be maneuvered around the site. Also the upfront investment of driving screws is only the price of a driver. Pneumatic nails are quick to drive and cheaper in bulk than screws ❷. The upfront cost includes not only the nailer but also the hose and compressor.

Hand-driving galvanized nails is frustrating because the metal is soft and the coating causes friction with the wood ❸. Unless you are an expert at hand-driving nails, you will bend a few before you are done, and the only thing harder than driving a galvanized nail without bending it is pulling it out without stripping the head off. Which method should you choose? Pick either of the first two but avoid hand-driving nails if you can.

❶

❷

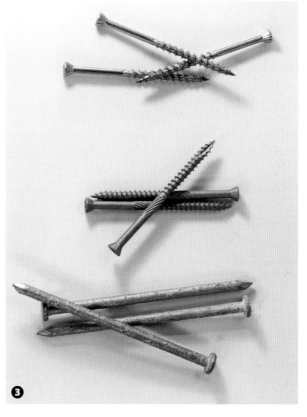

❸

LEVELS AND OTHER FRAMING TOOLS (CONTINUED)

TEN TOOLS YOU DIDN'T KNOW YOU NEEDED

As mentioned previously, you can build a deck with a very short list of tools, but if you have extra room in the budget, here are a few more items that will make the job easier.

A complete set of sockets comes in handy for attaching hardware and changing blades.

Right-angle grinders can be fitted for cutting or grinding and reach into tight places where other tools won't.

A rigger's hammer has a hatchet blade instead of a nail-pulling claw (and is the only hammer author Scott Grice will admit to owning).

Clamps are thought of as more of a woodworker's tool, but for those who typically work alone they're the cheapest extra hands you will find.

This big square replaces the need to pull a 3-4-5 triangle to get to square and it folds up neatly for easy storage.

Multi-tools have blossomed ever since the patent was released a few years ago; if you don't have one, go buy one.

Rubber bumpers on the ends of a post-hole digger will save your knuckles. This pair has offset handles as well for deeper digging.

Quarter-angle drills can fit into places a typical drill can't reach for both drilling and driving.

Construction calculators can work in inches and fractions and will calculate things like the area of a circle and the hypotenuse of a triangle.

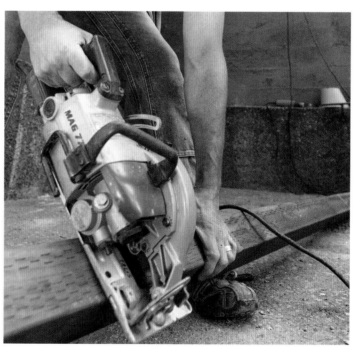

A rafter hook, a common accessory, will save your circular saw from being dropped. When not in use it folds out of the way.

FRAMING MATERIALS

Materials for framing a deck include not only the lumber (or steel) used for the structure but also the flashing, fasteners, and metal hardware that help establish and maintain the deck's structural integrity.

Framing lumber

The types of available framing lumber depend on your location. In the west, treated lumber is Douglas fir that has been incised to allow the chemical preservative to penetrate the wood. In the east, unincised treated yellow pine is prevalent. The uniformity of both kinds of framing lumber can be very inconsistent and understandably so. The pressure-treating process dramatically changes the wood's moisture percentage, which causes the boards to warp and twist. Not only will your lumber show up on the job warped, but it will also deflect once installed, as the moisture content acclimates to the environment.

To combat this continual wood movement, try to keep the lumber neatly stacked and out of the sun until it's installed. Once installed, don't leave the ends of posts or joists running wild for any length of time; otherwise, by the time you get around to attaching the other framing, the ends you left loose may be twisted out of alignment. Always wear gloves when handling pressure-treated lumber as the chemicals are toxic and any splinter you get will fester.

Incised pressure-treated wood (right) is darker and typically used in the western United States. Unincised yellow pine is common to the eastern United States.

Keep pressure-treated wood stacked with bands intact to retain the shape until time of use.

Wear gloves when handling pressure-treated lumber because the chemicals are toxic. Splinters can turn nasty.

After you frame a deck, you might want to hide the framing. This lattice is a common item on home-store shelves and does a nice job of dressing up the deck framing on this project.

It's recommended that you use dimensional lumber that is the full beam width rather than ganging together 2× material. Water collecting in the space between the boards could cause rot.

FRAMING WITH STEEL

An alternative to framing lumber is to frame your deck with cold-rolled, light-gauge galvanized steel joists. There are some solid advantages to steel framing: Steel joists are lighter than wood. The span capabilities of steel are greater than wood. Steel joists are flat and will stay that way, so there is no need to crown the joist before installation. Because steel joists are manufactured they can be made to a specific length; on a simple deck you could have all the joists show up ready to install.

But steel joists are not without their disadvantages. There is a learning curve to working with steel and some specialty tools are required. Cutting steel requires extra protection like a full face mask, long sleeves, and gloves so the hot steel doesn't burn you. You need to pay attention to where the steel bits created by the cuts are going. If left on the decking, they can cause stains; if shot into the yard, they can cut bare feet. Cut ends of steel joists need to be treated with zinc paint, very much

like the cut end of a pressure-treated board needs to be treated. Most builders incorporate wood posts into the steel frame because steel posts are an odd size, making it difficult to use standard post hardware. This means you'll have to fiddle with the post-to-steel connection.

This steel framing looks remarkably neat, because with steel there are no lumber imperfections to deal with.

Trex steel framing is a component system designed to require minimal modification of the steel parts. Sections of the infill and rim joists are shown here.

FRAMING MATERIALS (CONTINUED)

Framing hardware and fasteners

Framing hardware consists of connectors used to reinforce lumber connections to the house, foundation, or between framing members. Simpson® Strong-Tie® and USP Structural Connectors™ are the two dominant brands in the United States. Both have robust websites and catalogs to help you identify and choose the appropriate hardware for your project. While there are hardware options designed to strengthen every connection of a deck, such hardware is not necessarily required in each instance; check with your municipality for local code requirements. Some independent research will help you focus your hardware purchase to the needs of your specific job.

Key hardware connections To prevent deck failure, you'll need to do more than simply nail the deck together with 16d nails. To protect you, your family, or your clients from serious injury or death, there are a few key connections that must be done right (see "Roadmap to Hardware" at right).

➔ See "Resources," p. 216, for where to find more information on hardware connectors.

HOW HARDWARE IS TESTED

All new hardware products go through rigorous manufacturer testing before they are put on the market.

This pneumatic arm spends its days pulling apart structural mockups built by researchers at Simpson Strong-Tie. Here, the arm is testing the resistance to lateral load on a newel post.

This experiment is designed to test galvanic coatings against corrosion.

ROADMAP TO HARDWARE

Trying to pick deck hardware from a catalog can be bewildering. Remember that the hardware you need is dictated to a large degree by the lumber choices outlined in the deck design.

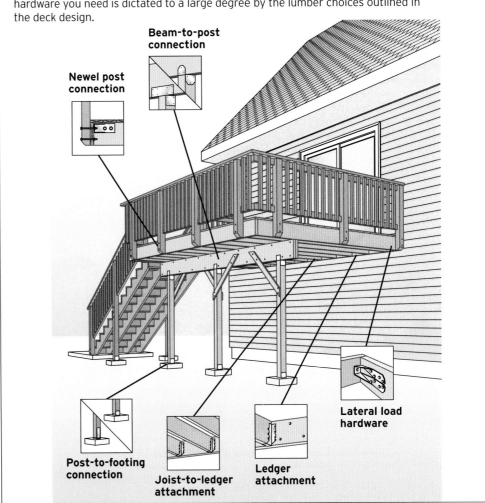

Beam-to-post connection

Newel post connection

Post-to-footing connection

Joist-to-ledger attachment

Ledger attachment

Lateral load hardware

Heavy-duty aluminum brackets can be used to create a stand-off space between the siding and deck structure to minimize siding interruption.

Joist hangers are matched to the joist or beam dimensions and transfer loads laterally between framing components.

Right-angle connectors reinforce joints to help keep the joist system solid.

Post-and-beam connectors ensure the integrity of the major framing components.

CONNECTING THE LEDGER TO THE HOUSE

The science of building is always evolving and one of the big changes (or clarifications, if you will) in recent years is how to attach the ledger to the house and how to protect the ledger against a lateral load failure—in other words, how to ensure that the ledger doesn't rip away from the house. To help prevent this, a deck ledger can be directly connected to the house's floor joists with tension ties. These ties are also used to secure newel posts against lateral loads. As the science continues to evolve, this current method of attachment will inevitably change.

LATERAL LOAD CONNECTORS SPAN TO THE HOUSE FRAMING

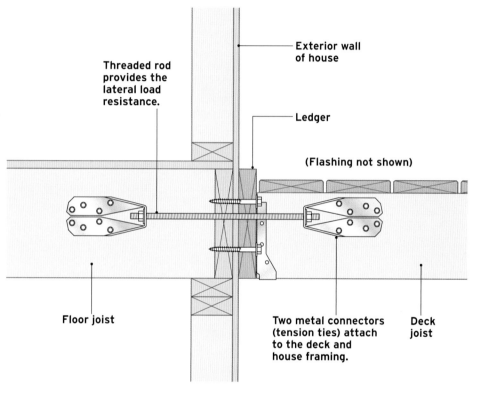

Exterior wall of house

Threaded rod provides the lateral load resistance.

Ledger

(Flashing not shown)

Floor joist

Two metal connectors (tension ties) attach to the deck and house framing.

Deck joist

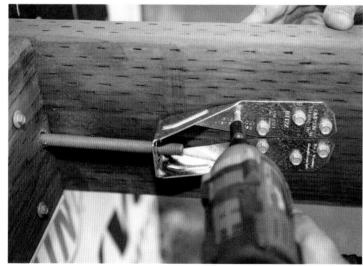

Tension ties tie the joists of the deck directly to the joists of the house, providing higher resistance to lateral loads.

FRAMING MATERIALS (CONTINUED)

Hex head (above top) and carriage head (above bottom) are two types of bolt heads you will commonly encounter.

FastenMaster's Thrulok bolt® (right) allows for speedy through-bolt connections with minimal fuss.

A star or Torx screw with a pan head (left) allows for maximum driving power without a washer.

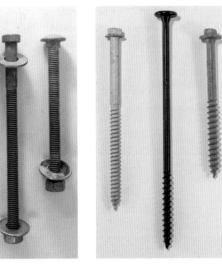

Substantial hardware often requires a wrench and socket set.

Many fasteners can be driven with a standard drill driver or impact driver.

Other assorted screws

Framing fasteners break down into four general categories: through bolts, lag screws, structural wood screws, and screws. Each type of fastener is meant for a particular connection, although some fasteners can serve double-duty, depending on the circumstances.

Flashing

If you've dismantled an old deck, you've probably had the opportunity to inspect areas of inadequate flashing. The vast majority of decks, especially if they were built more than a few years ago, are not properly flashed, yet we now know that proper flashing can have a huge effect on a deck's longevity. With the advent of self-adhesive membranes, the job of proper flashing has gotten much easier ❶. Be aware, however, there is a learning curve when working with this type of flashing—for example, the ability to consistently find the backing release cord ❷. If you decide to use metal flashing instead, you can choose coated aluminum, stainless steel, or copper ❸. The best flashing applications are often layered systems that combine self-adhesive membranes with metal flashing ❹.

➡ See "Installing Ledger Flashing," p. 98.

Whatever flashing situation you face, you will have a better chance of success if you assume that water will find a way in; the job of the flashing is to direct it back out again. That said, in extreme environments a strip of self-adhesive flashing applied over the joist top can provide the primary defense against water infiltration ❺. In this way, the flashing adds a protective layer between the decking's underside and the joist's top, closing a potential point of entry for rainwater ❻. Flashing also creates a seal around the fastener shank ❼ because the adhesive will stick to the screw as it penetrates the material ❽.

1 Self-adhesive flashing comes in rolls of varying widths and tackiness. In hot weather, choose a less aggressive adhesive.

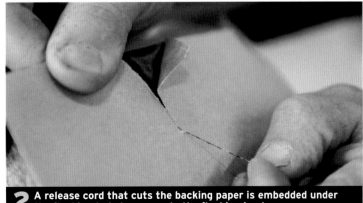

2 A release cord that cuts the backing paper is embedded under the flashing to help you apply the flashing in stages.

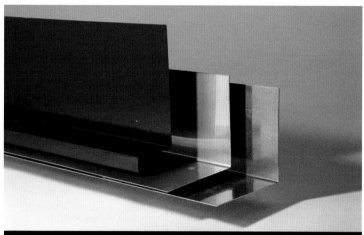

3 The composition of the metal flashing determines how well it will withstand the corrosive effects of the weather.

4 Layering flashing takes extra work up front but pays dividends down the road in avoiding expensive repairs.

5 Flashing the joist top prevents water from penetrating into the middle of the joist, where there is less chemical protection.

6 Seen in cutaway, flashing applied over the top of the joist seals the fastener shank.

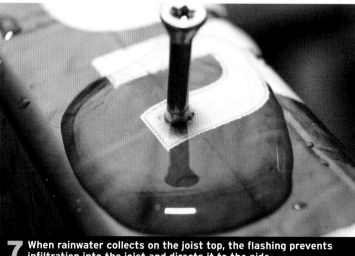

7 When rainwater collects on the joist top, the flashing prevents infiltration into the joist and directs it to the side.

8 The gooey flashing adhesive seals around the shank as it is driven in.

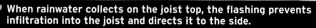

DECKING TOOLS

You can get away with installing the decking with the tools used for framing, but there are some optional items that will make the job easier. Careful technique with a circular saw enables you to cut all the decking to length, although a good chopsaw, set to the right height, will save your back and likely produce better results. To avoid splitting the decking or breaking screws, be sure to drill pilot holes **❶**. You can save some time by using two drivers instead of changing the bit each time you need to switch between driving and drilling **❷**.

➡ **See "Setting Up a Cut Station," p. 154.**

Cut ends need to be rounded, and for softwoods a rough rasp does the trick with a few swipes. For hardwood, however, a trim router fitted with a ¼-in. roundover bit is much faster than a rasp **❸**. Note that some fastening systems, such as Kreg's, require proprietary tools **❹**. Other tools that come in handy are pipe clamps and a small prybar to move boards into alignment and a jigsaw for fitting decking around posts and door thresholds **❺**.

➡ **See "Installing Deck Planks," p. 156.**

1 This two-in-one bit makes a pilot hole and a countersink at the same time. The adjustable collar sets the depth of the hole.

2 Not only does dedicating an extra driver for a pilot bit save time, but it also saves wear and tear on the chuck.

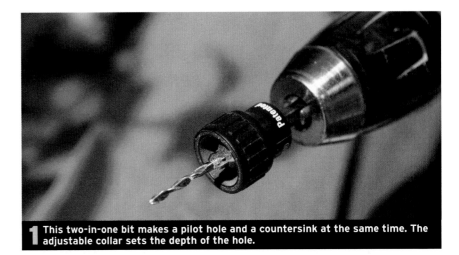

3 When installing hardwood decking, a trim router fitted with a ¼-in. roundover bit does a better job than a rasp.

Using a cat's paw and a small block of wood is a simple and quick technique for minor decking adjustments. Protect the decking's edge with the wood block, pound the cat's paw into the joist, and pry the decking into place.

A wood wedge has a sharp metal U that bites into the joist as it is pounded down. The wedge works well, but varying lumber thicknesses can be a problem.

While it looks more medieval than modern, this cam-system adjuster is surprisingly efficient but carries a hefty price tag.

THREE TOOLS FOR PRYING DECKING

4 The Kreg jig system is an innovative hidden fastener design that guides a toe-screw and doesn't rely on clips, tongs, or teeth.

5 Attention to details often defines the quality of the deck. Here, a jigsaw was used to carefully fit the decking around a post.

DECKING MATERIALS

1 Some common softwood decking types are untreated cedar, pressure-treated softwood, and untreated Douglas fir, which must be protected with a finish and maintained regularly.

2 Exotic hardwoods can be finished or left unfinished. Look for sustainably harvested certified decking.

3 This sample of thermally modified wood (the dark wood in the center) is nearly indistinguishable from the hardwood that surrounds it.

4 Capstock decking (the bottom two samples) has a plastic core.

5 The future of natural decking: Resysta® is engineered from rice husks, salt, and mineral oil.

When Trex® composite decking was widely introduced to the market nearly 20 years ago, those of us working in the building trades could feel our world shake a bit. It was exciting to think that milk bottles and sawdust could be baked into a premium homebuilding product. The evolution of composite decking from then to now hasn't been without some bumps, but today the industry is in its prime, with innovative technologies and increased demand driving new products. Today the offerings of both composites and wood decking are nearly unrecognizable compared to what they were when Trex first came onto the market.

Decking materials can be split into the two broad categories of wood and synthetic,

each of which contains several options. Wood, the traditional choice for decking, is available in **1** naturally rot- and insect-resistant softwoods, chemically treated softwoods, and **2** exotic hardwoods. A relatively new category of nonchemically treated wood can best be described as "cooked" wood because the lumber has been baked, salted, or infused with vinegar to make it rot and pest resistant **3**.

Synthetic decking is composed of either a mix of wood and plastic or all plastic. A new variation of modern decking is capstock, in which a thin layer of dense, textured plastic surrounds a lighter plastic core **4**. Although Trex was the first company to introduce an alternative to wood decking, other manufac-

turers quickly developed their own synthetic building products **5**.

A third category includes metal and stone decking, which seem to stretch the very definition of a deck. These systems sometimes require special framing (especially with stone) and might challenge your belief that you are at home instead of standing on the deck of a ship. However, if you have a large budget and no time for upkeep, you might consider these durable, low-maintenance options.

➔ **For information on finishing materials, see "Working with Finishes," p. 210.**

This pressure-treated decking, installed in a herringbone pattern, will resist rot and is an increasingly popular choice for hot, humid climates. Pressure-treated decking is typically not rated for ground contact and some brands claim not to be any more corrosive than untreated decking. Although a less expensive option, pressure-treated decking has a reputation for twisting and checking after it's installed.

FINISH OR LET IT GO GRAY?

These two decks of nearly identical hardwoods looked similar when installed. The finished deck is on a regular maintenance schedule, which includes washing and refinishing. The unfinished deck has been left to go gray but is still maintained with regular washings to prevent a buildup of mildew.

WHAT CAN GO WRONG

Hardwood tends to check. Despite being regularly maintained, this hardwood stair stringer checked after installation. While the stringer is still structurally sound, not everyone will like the look.

FOOTINGS AND FOUNDATIONS

MOST OF THE HARD WORK IN creating footings is in the planning, preparation, and layout. Digging and pouring concrete get all the attention, but by the time you pick up the shovel most of the work is already done. Anyone can dig a hole. It's also critical for the success and longevity of your project that the foundation planning is done correctly. And while what's visible of a foundation belies the work that goes into it, if done poorly, any passerby can see the results of a poor foundation in the crooked and sagging deck that is the result.

In this chapter you'll learn how to calculate the overall load of the deck and how to divide that load equally among the footings. After that, we'll go through the steps of layout, excavation, and installation for a variety of footing types. This chapter covers the basics of the installation process. For more on design and footing types, see "Designing a Deck" on p. 6.

PRACTICAL CONSIDERATIONS

Digging the footings for the deck will be the messiest part of the entire project. You can't escape the fact that you are digging in the dirt. Even if you don't use heavy equipment like a backhoe or skid loader, tracking dirt around with your boots and a wheelbarrow can do a number on the lawn. If the only access to the digging area is over the lawn, consider throwing down some plywood or planking. As long as the lawn is covered for only a few days, it should spring back and be better for the protection. If excavation equipment is involved, putting down some planks for the equipment to drive over may help a little, depending on the equipment size. Where possible, consider digging at a time when the ground is not soaked. If there's an irrigation system, turn it off a few days before to let the ground dry out.

Before the dirt is out of the hole you need to arrange a place to put it. If some of the backfill is needed for around the footings once they are poured, then piling it on plywood serves the purpose (use a tarp under the plywood for extra protection if you're working on the lawn). If the footprint of the deck itself will hide the damage to the yard, then there is no need for plywood or tarps. In this case, simply backfill where you need to after installing the footings and spread the excess dirt out evenly under the deck's footprint.

FROST HEAVE WILL WREAK HAVOC ON YOUR DECK

Frost heave occurs when freezing temperatures penetrate the ground and cause subsurface water to form ice lenses that displace the soil and anything that rests on or in it. This is why it is important to extend the footings of your deck below the frost line. If the footings aren't deep enough, frost heave will lift them in unpredictable ways.

As the footing moves, the wooden structure above kinks and rotates, straining the joints of the deck. This strain usually eases when the soil thaws and the deck settles again. But the damage has been done and the affected joints have been compromised; your deck is no longer as stable as it was and moves a bit when people walk across it. Play this scenario out over a number of years and it is easy to see that a little bit of frost heave can have profound effects on the structural integrity of the deck.

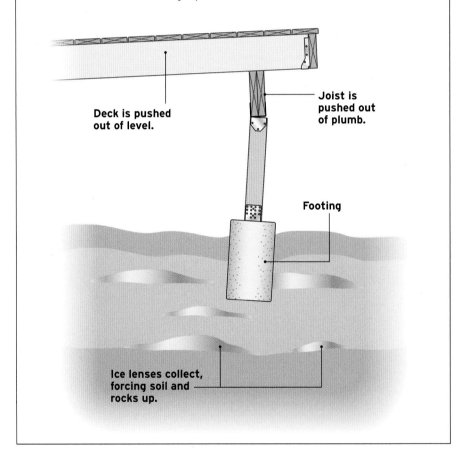

Deck is pushed out of level.

Joist is pushed out of plumb.

Footing

Ice lenses collect, forcing soil and rocks up.

Before you dig

There will be some staging to do of foundation materials like concrete bags, gravel, rebar, and forms, so you'll want to establish this area before starting the project. The driveway is a popular spot for staging because the surface is durable and generally easy to clean up. It's also an easy spot for a delivery drop. If you can't stage in the driveway or want to consolidate materials closer to the work zone, again, consider throwing down some plywood. Plywood will not only protect the lawn but also help prevent bagged concrete mix and cardboard forms from absorbing the ground moisture.

A little investigation can save a lot of frustration. If you are unsure of how easy (or hard) the excavation will be, dig a test hole a few days before. Give yourself enough time between digging a test hole and the scheduled start of the project to rent equipment or arrange some help if need be. Wasting the time you scheduled for digging by running around trying to scare up some help for a difficult excavation is a good prescription for premature graying.

Where possible, **stage heavy objects off the ground—both to save energy and to help keep your back in good working order.**

You never know what you might find. We knew the ground on this job might be a little rocky, but in this particular footing hole we found almost nothing but 5-in. to 10-in. angular rocks presumably dumped as backfill when the house was built 50 years earlier. As a result, digging this hole took about three times as long as we'd anticipated.

WARNING

Call before you dig! Finding a utility line by accident is a reliable way to ruin your day. Luckily, there is a number you can call from anywhere in the country that will help you avoid discovering a utility line in the wrong way. Call 811 or visit www.call811.com to, as they say, know what's below.

WHAT YOU'LL NEED

- Shovel
- Pick
- Post-hole digger
- Excavator (if necessary)
- Marking spray
- String line
- Long measuring tape
- Gloves
- Wheelbarrow
- Concrete mix
- Rebar
- Water

CALCULATING FOOTING SIZE

Calculating footing size has to do with a number of variables, including the size of the deck, how many footings you want to use, the deck design, where in the country you live, and factors like soil type and site slope. There is a lot of information that goes in to calculating the size and configuration of footings and some of that information is beyond the scope of this book. That said, general rules apply to just about every footing, and learning these basic concepts will get you well down the road to understanding footing requirements. The drawing below outlines how to estimate footing load based on deck size and framing configuration–namely beam placement.

➡ For more information on footing design, see "Foundations," p. 23.

CALCULATING LOAD TO ESTIMATE FOOTING SIZE

Tributary load is the weight of all uniform, live, and dead loads of the deck that are supported by an individual component of the deck structure. To determine tributary load, follow these steps:

1. Calculate the overall weight of the deck. The standard load for decks is 50 lb. per square foot (10 lb. of dead load, 40 lb. of live load). So for a deck that is 100 sq. ft. the total load is 5,000 lb.

2. Determine the bearing capacity of the soil. You can hire a geologist to do this or check with your local building department, which usually has set default bearing capacities for your area. In our neck of the woods, the bearing capacity of the soil is rated at 1,500 lb. per square foot.

3. Now you need to determine how you are going to channel the weight of the deck to the ground. The deck shown here is a simple rectangle with a ledger attachment to the house. A beam carries the other side of the deck. The ledger transfers some of the weight of the deck to the house, but how much? By dividing the joist span from the ledger to the beam by half we get 4 ft. Multiplying 4 ft. by the entire 10-ft. run of the ledger, we get the total square footage that the ledger must carry: 40 sq. ft. So the tributary load on the ledger is 2,000 lb.

4. This leaves 3,000 lb. of load that must be transferred to the ground by means of the posts and footings. (The beam carries more because the joists cantilever over the top of the beam.) In the example shown here there are three posts. How much load will each post carry? We know that the joist span loaded on the posts is 6 ft., the overall joist span is 10 ft., and the ledger is picking up 4 of those feet. The missing piece of information is how much of the beam span each post is picking up.

5. Measuring the distance from post to post and dividing by two determines the beam span loaded on each post. The distance between each post is 5 ft. So for the end posts the total load is 15 sq. ft. (2.5 ft. times 6 ft.), or 750 lb. The middle post, because it has posts on either side, carries twice the amount of the end posts–that is, 1,500 lb.

6. We know the load bearing on each post. We also know the bearing capacity of the soil. Now we can calculate what size the footings need to be. The middle post needs a footing that is 1 sq. ft. in bearing area (1,500 divided by 1,500). The end posts need a bearing area half that size (750 divided by 1,500).

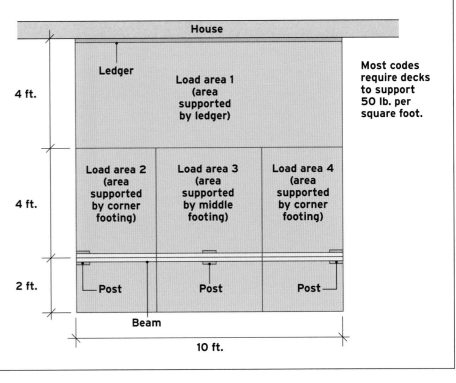

House

Ledger

4 ft.

Load area 1 (area supported by ledger)

Most codes require decks to support 50 lb. per square foot.

4 ft.

Load area 2 (area supported by corner footing)

Load area 3 (area supported by middle footing)

Load area 4 (area supported by corner footing)

2 ft.

Post · Post · Post

Beam

10 ft.

ESTABLISHING CONTROL LINES

1 Measure out from the ledger wall to establish a parallel line along the ground.

2 Secure the control line at one end at a known measurement.

3 String a control line from the fixed point to the batter board.

4 Adjust the string until it is plumb over the parallel line marked on the ground.

5 Mark the string's location so it can be removed and then reliably put back.

Establishing control lines is a way to create order out of the chaos of an unmarked construction site. Control lines are not lines painted on the ground but rather string lines stretched between fixed locations. The strings can be put up when you need them for reference or taken down when work is in progress. The strings can be secured to anything that is stable for the duration of the job. If there is nothing on site to tie the string to, it's a good idea to erect a batter board; two stakes set in the ground a foot apart with a third stake screwed horizontally between them (see the top photo on p. 72). For the job shown here, we used part of the previous deck's steel framing to fix the control line to. Typically two control lines running perpendicular to each other are sufficient (see the drawing on p. 72).

One control line runs parallel to the major framing elements, such as the supporting ledger and the main beams. For this deck, we checked the main wall of the house for plumb and straight and because it was within 1/2 in. we used that as a reference to set the main control line **1**. A control line can be established independent of the framing elements, along the center of the framing elements, or along one edge. We like to align the control line with the leading edge of a run of posts.

A control line doesn't have to be a string line. If the deck is built into the corner of a house, as on this job, you can use one wall of the house as the second control line that runs perpendicular to the first. To do this, check the walls for square using the 3-4-5 method (see "Squaring with the 3-4-5 Method" on p. 72).

Once you've established that the two walls are at 90° to each other, measure out from the primary wall the distance to the control line—in this case, equal to the distance from the wall to the leading edge of the first run of posts **2**. This is one end of the parallel control line.

The elevation of the string is your preference. On this job, a foundation wall projected out a few inches so this ledge was a natural place to locate the string **3**. In an ideal world, you'll want to locate the string a few inches above the finished height of the footings. This will make it easy to verify alignment with a small square instead of using a level. Plumb down from the string line to mark key locations on the ground **4**. Mark the string position along the batter board (in this case the steel framing) **5**. Once the control line is located, you can use it to locate most of the deck's major elements.

ESTABLISHING CONTROL LINES (CONTINUED)

LOCATING CONTROL LINES

There is no hard-and-fast rule about where to position the control lines. The objective is to put them where they will be most helpful and where you can repeatedly set them up in the same spot whenever you need them for reference. Generally, there are two control lines that run perpendicular to each other: one parallel to the major beams and one parallel to the joists.

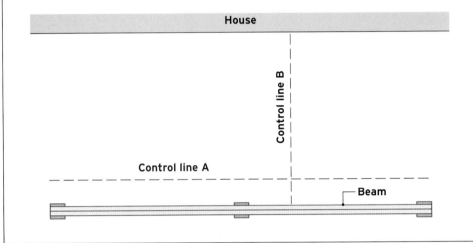

Batter boards are horizontal boards nailed to posts placed just outside the corners of the deck perimeter. They provide an easy way to establish the control lines used for layout.

SQUARING WITH THE 3-4-5 METHOD

Simple geometry and a tape measure allow you to establish a 90° angle. Use any multiples of 3-4-5.

1. Measure and mark 6 ft. on one side of the 90° angle.

2. Measure and mark 8 ft. on the other side of the 90° angle.

3. Measure from the first mark to the second mark.

4. A 90° triangle will have a 10-ft. hypotenuse.

LOCATING THE FOOTINGS

1 Locate each footing by measuring the distance and plumbing down with a level.

2 Mark plumb under the control line at each end to mark a run of footings.

3 Snap a chalkline under the control line to use as a reference to locate the footings.

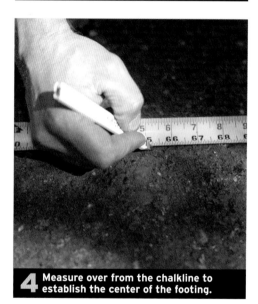

4 Measure over from the chalkline to establish the center of the footing.

5 Measure the footing's perimeter based on the calculations of footing size.

6 Mark the footing perimeter once the location and size are determined.

Determining where to dig a footing is fairly forgiving because if you are a little off, you can always adjust the hole. That said, locating the footing precisely saves on concrete because the hole will be the right size, instead of oversize.

Locating footings under the control line takes only a few steps. If the grade is uneven or won't take a chalkline, you'll have to locate each footing separately **1**. But if you're working on a concrete slab (as shown in the photos), it's easy to establish marks under the control line **2**. Simply plumb down from each end, make a mark, and snap a chalkline between the marks **3**. For each footing along the run, use the chalkline as a reference and mark its center **4**. Then use that center point as a reference to measure the footing's perimeter **5**.

By now you might be asking why this level of meticulousness is necessary. After all, you're just marking out a footing. It's true that the process is pretty straightforward; however, getting it wrong has some pretty weighty consequences. First, if you happen to get a persnickety inspector, being off only 1 in. in footing size could mean the difference between a passed inspection and having to repour the concrete. Second, and more important, being laissez-faire about footing installation can lead to an inferior deck. The last step is to mark the footing's perimeter by connecting the dots **6**.

LOCATING THE FOOTINGS (CONTINUED)

1 Use a tape measure and string line to locate the center of the footing and spray a mark at that point.

2 Center the footing form over the mark to determine the outer perimeter of the finished form.

Locating footings on an uneven grade

Most of the time, footings will need to be installed in rough, uneven terrain. In this situation, the method for locating the footings is slightly less precise but faster. As with the method just described, you'll use a string line for reference. The string should be set up so it's plumb under the center of the beam. The string does not need to be set level; instead, place it as close to grade as possible so you can eyeball from the string plumb to the ground **1**. Once all the footing positions are marked with an X, center a section of the appropriate-size footing form over the mark **2**. Then use marking spray to outline the base of the form **3**. After you remove the form, the outline of its location should be clearly visible **4**. The hole you'll dig needs to be about 2 in. larger than the outline on all sides **5**. Mark the diameter of the hole. Notice that we made our markings square; you can make them round but we like to make them square and leave the outside corners to give us some points of reference as we dig **6**.

3 Mark the ground outside the footing form to give yourself a reference to mark the perimeter to excavate.

4 Check the center mark's location in relation to the perimeter to make sure the form is placed where you want it.

5 Mark 2 in. outside the form's perimeter to indicate the excavation line.

6 Complete the excavation perimeter by connecting the lines to make either a square or a circular outline.

POURING A BASIC FOOTING

1 Excavate the foundation but remember to leave the perimeter markings to guide the digging progress.

2 Dig the hole at least 2 in. deeper than the required minimum for gravel.

3 Fill the bottom 2 in. of the hole with gravel to drain water and prevent frost heave.

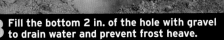

4 Compact the drainage gravel to provide a solid support for the footing and help prevent the footing from settling over time.

Preparations for footing installation can be as simple as grabbing a shovel and measuring tape. How far down you need to dig depends on the region in which you live and the specific soil type you have. In fact, there are large swaths of the country where scratching out a flat spot and adding some gravel will do the trick. However, if you are building in a region that has cold winter weather, you'll need to excavate to avoid the potential of frost heave.

Under perfect conditions, installing a pier footing is relatively easy and can take as little as 20 minutes from the start of digging to finishing the concrete. You'll have to decide for yourself how far your situation is removed from perfect, but once you've installed the first footing you'll at least have a baseline to estimate how long it will take to install the remaining footings. Whether you dig all the footings at once before mixing any concrete or whether you complete

TRADE SECRET

Where a significant amount of digging is required, either by code or the size of the deck, consider renting a small backhoe. Most equipment-rental outlets rent small skid loaders with backhoe attachments that don't require a special license to operate.

5 Set up a reference line over the hole, registered on the centerline of the beam.

6 Adjust the string close to grade so you can use it for reference.

7 Mark the form for whatever portion of the footing will protrude above grade.

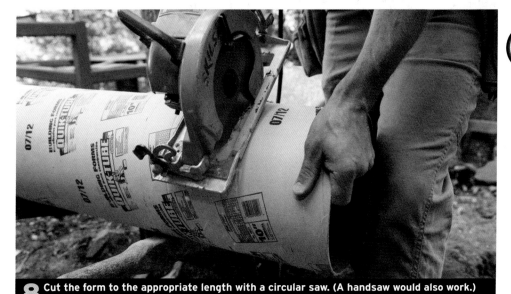

8 Cut the form to the appropriate length with a circular saw. (A handsaw would also work.)

WHAT CAN GO WRONG

Digging is not always easy, especially when you encounter rocks, roots, or other obstacles. With large rocks, you will have to make a judgment call about whether it is better to work around them or remove them. Roots, on the other hand, must be removed.

each footing before moving on to the next is a matter of personal preference ❶.

When digging a footing, resist the urge to stop at the minimum depth required by code ❷. First, there is a tendency to measure from the deepest place in the hole, typically the center, and angle the tape to the side, which overestimates the true depth of the hole. Second, it's a good idea to put a 2-in. layer of drainage gravel in the bottom of the hole ❸. Using a gravel tamper is one

way to compact the drainage gravel to prevent settling issues. However, a 200-lb. helper can be just as effective ❹. The helper method doesn't work as well if the area to be compacted is larger than a couple square feet.

A cardboard tube form is a good way to finish a footing top. To gauge the length of form needed, set up the string line used initially to locate the footing ❺. Measuring from the string to grade will provide a

POURING A BASIC FOOTING (CONTINUED)

9 Add concrete to the hole until it comes up to the surrounding finished grade.

10 Agitate the concrete with a shovel to remove any air pockets.

11 Flatten the top of the concrete. It does not need to be smooth at this stage.

12 Place the footing form on the concrete and level it in both directions.

13 Fill the footing form with concrete and smooth the top with a trowel.

14 Double-check the footing location by setting up the string line.

rough estimate of the needed form length **6** (p. 77). Mark the form in multiple locations to guide the cut **7** (p. 77). You can cut the cardboard forms with a handsaw, but the job will go more quickly if you have a circular saw handy **8** (p. 77).

If you have only one footing, or even several shallow footings, it's easiest and least expensive to prepare bag-mixed concrete in a wheelbarrow **9**. Even if the job is big enough to justify getting concrete delivered, chances are the concrete will need to

be transported in a wheelbarrow from the truck to the footing hole. The mix should be a medium consistency; a little dry but wet enough to easily conform to the hole with a little agitation **10**. When the concrete is even, or a little below grade, level the surface with a float **11**. At this stage the concrete just needs to be flat, not smooth. In fact, leaving it a little rough will help the base of the footing bond to the tube portion. Use the string as a guide to level and center the segment of footing form **12**. Shovel

more concrete into the form and agitate it to ensure a good concrete bond. Once filled, trowel the top of the footing smooth **13**. Before letting the concrete set, double-check the position to make sure the form did not move off alignment **14**. Some types of post-base hardware are set into wet concrete, which you would add at this stage.

➔ See "Working with Concrete," p. 45.

POURING FOOTINGS IN A PATIO

There are times when it makes sense to put footings in an existing patio (after all, there's enough building detritus in the world without adding to it). Working through a concrete pad requires a few extra tools, such as a masonry blade fitted to a typical circular saw. If you have a lot of footings to install, you might want to rent a roller attachment that fixes to the saw's foot so the saw can easily travel along the cut line ❶. A heavy-duty prybar will definitely come in handy to cut roots or pry out released concrete ❷. In addition, a maul or sledgehammer will be indispensable. An item you might not expect to need is an ax for cutting any roots that have wandered under the concrete ❸. Note that the latest post-hole diggers have been designed to make digging deep holes in tight spaces much easier if not enjoyable ❹. Once the hole is dug, prepare it for concrete like any typical footing by packing 2 in. of gravel into the bottom ❺. Once the footing is filled with concrete, use a trowel to finish the surface flush to the existing patio ❻.

1 Cut the concrete patio with a circular saw fitted with a masonry blade.

2 Use a prybar to remove the concrete in the footing location.

3 Remove any roots, rocks, or other debris that will affect the integrity of the footing.

4 Dig down below the frost level determined by your local code.

5 Add 2 in. of compacted gravel to the bottom of the footing excavation to help with drainage.

6 Add concrete until it is even with the existing patio, agitate, and smooth the top.

ⓘ WHAT CAN GO WRONG

Old concrete slabs typically come in two thicknesses: too thin and too thick. Most concrete gets harder as it ages, so thick concrete plus a bunch of years equals a stubborn slab that may require a jackhammer to remove.

INSTALLING FOOTING HARDWARE

There are generally two ways to install footing hardware: either while the concrete is still wet or once it has set. Wet-setting hardware has the advantage that there is no drilling or application of epoxy. However, there is a limited amount of time to get the placement perfect. Dry-setting hardware in footings is just the opposite. You'll have all the time you want, but drilling out the hole and setting the bolt with epoxy can be an aggravating process. Also there are fewer hardware options that are designed for dry setting.

Wet-setting hardware

As mentioned, the main challenge in wet-setting foundation hardware is quickly locating the hardware exactly where it needs to go; depending on the juiciness of the concrete mix, getting the hardware to stay put while the concrete sets can present an additional challenge. A simple alignment technique is to position a board to register the hardware against ❶. Align the board to the edge of the post run and install all the hardware with one edge touching the board ❷. Depending on the weight of the board, you may have to secure it temporarily by tacking the board to the blocks. After about 5 minutes, check the hardware to make sure that is has not shifted or sagged off alignment ❸.

1 Set the post base's anchor in the wet concrete aligned with the layout line.

2 Use a straight board aligned with the edge of the run of posts as a positive stop to position the post bases.

3 Check the position after 5 minutes to make sure the post base has not shifted out of position. If necessary, attach it to the alignment board.

WHAT CAN GO WRONG

Some battery-operated drivers have a hammer-drill setting, and you might be able to drill one hole with them. But if you've got a series of holes to bore, the likelihood of burning out the motor is high. Better to rent a hammer drill that can handle the job. Masonry bits can be rented as well, but it is usually more economical to buy one.

1 Locate the bolt's center mark using the post base's attachment plate.

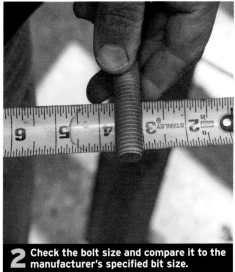

2 Check the bolt size and compare it to the manufacturer's specified bit size.

3 Bore the bolt hole using a masonry bit and a heavy-duty hammer drill.

4 Adjust the compressor to 120 psi.

5 Use an air nozzle to blow the masonry dust out of the hole.

6 Loosen any lingering dust with a reamer brush and remove it with compressed air.

Dry-setting hardware

To dry-set hardware, let the concrete cure for at least 24 hours (drilling green concrete runs the risk of cracking it). Most attachment hardware systems have a plate or washer that the bolt slides through. This plate can be used to locate where to drill the bolt hole **1**. When drilling for a $5/8$-in. bolt, make the hole slightly oversize; otherwise, the dust and debris in the hole will clog the bolt and not allow it to set fully in the hole **2**. Hardware manufacturers will specify the appropriate size bolt and hole for their specific hardware. When drilling, it's a good idea to lift the bit partway up out of the hole to clear some of the dust off the drill shank **3**.

Once the hole is bored, there is a fairly detailed protocol for securing the bolt with epoxy. There is also a specific set of tools to buy or rent, including an air compressor, a hole brush, and an air nozzle attachment. First, the hole needs to be cleared of dust by blowing in air compressed at 120 psi **4**. A common air compressor fitted with an air nozzle will work just fine. Be prepared for a plume of dust to rush out of the hole with the first blast of air **5**. After blowing out the hole, ream it with an appropriately sized

INSTALLING FOOTING HARDWARE (CONTINUED)

7 Mix the two-part epoxy by passing it through a mixing-tube applicator.

8 Run a small sample line to check that the epoxy is adequately mixed.

Apply the epoxy by inserting the nozzle into the hole and filling from the bottom.

9

10 Insert the bolt and plunge it several times to work the epoxy up the sides.

11 Hold the bolt fully plunged for a few seconds to allow the epoxy to relax.

12 Remove any excess epoxy before it dries.

brush ❻ (p. 81). Repeat this process a couple of times to make sure the hole is clean so that the epoxy will bond.

Two-part epoxy enters the mixing tube as separate black and white elements and mixes as it progresses down the tube ❼. It should be an even gray when it exits the end of the tube, which indicates that it's thoroughly mixed ❽. The applicator tube should be of a small enough diameter to allow you to insert the tube into the bolt hole and apply the epoxy up from the bottom of the hole ❾. The first time you insert the bolt it will want to spring back up because of the epoxy's elasticity. To avoid this springback, plunge the bolt until the epoxy has worked up the sides of the hole and the bolt shank ❿. Then, if necessary, hold the bolt down until it decides it wants to stay. Note that the nut should be threaded on during this process ⓫. The nut provides a handle to work the bolt with and also protects the threads from getting gooped up with excess epoxy ⓬. While the epoxy is still pliable, scrape away any excess from around the bolt that might prevent the post base from fully resting on the footing surface.

TRADE SECRET

Keep the dust out. To prevent masonry dust from effectively shortening the hole you just bored, wipe it away before you remove the bit.

INSTALLING A GRADE BEAM

There are many situations where a standard footing just won't do the job. Grade beams and landing pads with integral footings are two ways to upgrade a footing's appearance. For multistory decks, decks that support hot tubs, and decks on a severe slope, the footings may need to be drawn by a certified architect or engineer. There are also off-the-shelf footing forms, form additions, and concrete reinforcements that are readily available at home stores.

➡ See also "Nonconcrete Options and Precast Piers," p. 49.

A good option for support at the base of a stairs is to install a grade beam, which is essentially a short foundation wall that supports both newel posts and the weight of the stairs. The main advantage of a grade beam is its low profile. It's easily hidden under the bottom step, so, while the stairs are fully supported, you can incorporate the landscaping you want. For example, you could install grass or gravel flush to the bottom riser. Or at a later date you could install a landing pad independent of the stair support.

Building the form

A method we have found works well is to align the form in its final position, and then use that to locate where to dig. To do this, cut the stringers with the appropriate rise and run and then temporarily secure them in their final location ❶ (p. 84). With this method, we let the soil constrain the concrete for the majority of the grade beam and form only the top few inches. Depending on the soil quality for your particular project, you may have to excavate a larger area and extend the form sides down the full height of the grade beam.

If you want the finished riser to conceal the concrete, use the front of the rough stringer to align the inside, front form board ❷ (p. 84). Using steel stakes to secure the form is a big advantage over wooden stakes cut on the spot because they have a relatively small diameter, which will displace less soil, making them easier to drive ❸ (p. 84). Also,

the tip of the stake is in line with the shaft, unlike a roughly cut stake where the point may be off center. These two factors make it much easier to drive a steel stake straight down. Assemble the form using the stakes to hold the boards in position ❹ (p. 84).

➡ See "Deck Stairs," p. 190.

A small form like the one shown in the photos on p. 84 does not need to resist much pressure from the weight of the concrete. However, as the form size increases, the weight of the concrete will put a surprising amount of pressure on the form and can easily blow out poorly fastened joints or form boards. When securing the form sides, consider the direction the concrete will push ❺ (p. 84). Because the grade beam is hidden in front and must stop before the first riser, add volume to the back and depth of

the concrete to gain the adequate size to support the stairs ❻ (p. 84). Once you're satisfied with the form, mark the outside with marking spray ❼ (p. 85), which leaves a reference line for excavating the footing ❽ (p. 85). If you mark the inside, you would remove the reference line as you dig.

Pouring the grade beam

As with a typical footing, the depth of a grade beam must extend below the frost depth plus a couple inches to allow room for drainage gravel at the bottom ❾ (p. 85). On this project, we used a very coarse drainage gravel left over from another project, so using a soil tamper was a better choice than trying to stomp the gravel down ❿ (p. 85). A simple rebar frame will add considerable strength to

(Continued on p. 87)

LANDING PAD FOR STAIRS

For high-traffic stairs, a concrete landing pad provides a durable, dependable area that can handle the foot traffic. What makes a concrete pad for stairs different from a pad in another high-traffic zone, such as outside a garage door, is that a stair pad incorporates support for the taking the weight of the stair framing as well as structural support for the newel posts at the bottom of the stair run.

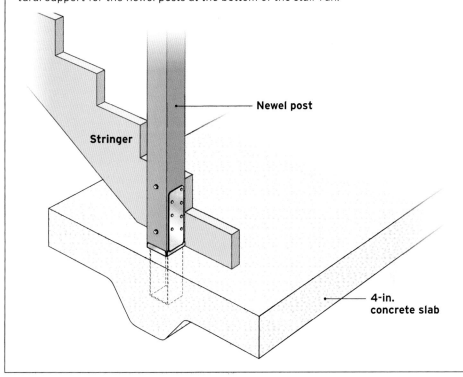

Newel post

Stringer

4-in. concrete slab

INSTALLING A GRADE BEAM (CONTINUED)

1 Place cut stringers in their final position by temporarily attaching the tops and resting them on blocks at the bottom.

2 Align the front of the form with the leading edge of the stair stringer to ensure that the grade beam will be hidden.

3 Install stakes on the outside of the form to hold the front form board in place.

4 Place all the form boards to complete the form perimeter. In this case, only three boards were needed.

5 Secure the form parts with 3-in. screws.

6 Double-check to make sure that the form is aligned correctly when the form stakes are installed.

7 Spray the ground to indicate the outside perimeter of the form boards.

8 Excavate the dirt from the foundation footprint. Leave the marked line to use as a reference while digging.

9 Dig down 2 in. below frost depth as determined by your local building department.

10 Add and compact 2 in. of drainage gravel at the bottom of the footing to help prevent frost heave.

11 Cut lengths of rebar 4 in. shorter than the overall footing length and 2 in. shorter than the overall height.

12 Use rebar ties to connect the rebar frame. For a small footing like this, the exact configuration is not critical.

INSTALLING A GRADE BEAM (CONTINUED)

13 Hand mix the concrete until it has the consistency of thick cottage cheese.

14 Tap the rebar frame into position once there are a few inches of concrete in the footing.

15 Agitate the concrete to eliminate air pockets that could weaken the footing.

16 Place the form in the position established by the steel stakes.

17 Align the top of the form with the top of the stakes. If necessary, use gravel or concrete to hold the form in place.

18 Reposition the stringer; and if necessary, attach supports.

19 Level the form and secure it in place by screwing it to the steel stakes.

20 Fill the form to the top with concrete, agitating the concrete as you progress.

21 Finish the top to your satisfaction. The top needs to be flat, but not pretty.

TRADE SECRET

When positioning the forms and stakes, align the stakes and form tops flush to the top of the finished concrete height. When the form is positioned after excavation there will be an easy place to register to location and the tops of the stakes won't get in the way when you're finishing the concrete.

the concrete. To estimate the length, place the rebar in the excavated trench and eyeball a cut 4 in. shorter than the trench. Use an angle grinder fitted with an abrasive blade to make the cut **11** (p. 85). Then cut vertical rebar sections a couple of inches shorter than the overall grade-beam depth and hold the frame together with rebar wire ties **12** (p. 85). For a single grade beam, you'll want to prepare concrete bag mix in a wheelbarrow adjacent to the site **13**. Add a few inches of mixed concrete to the trench and tap the rebar into position **14**. Avoid sinking the vertical rebar legs into the soil as this may provide a pathway for rust, eventually

weakening the overall structure. Mix and add more concrete, being sure to agitate the mix to eliminate any air pockets **15**.

When the concrete is near grade, place the form in position **16** by aligning the form's top with the steel stakes **17**. At this point, it's a good idea to place a stringer in position to fine-tune the grade beam's alignment **18**. Also level the form's top while securing the form to the stakes to ensure the form doesn't shift out of position **19**. With the form secure, fill concrete to the top, remembering to agitate the mix **20**. Using the form to guide the float, smooth the top of the grade beam to a rough finish **21**.

FRAMING A DECK

DECK FRAMING IS DEMANDING. The lumber is heavy, the job site can be difficult to maneuver in, and everything, including the carpenter, is exposed to the weather. Framing is known as "rough" carpentry because appearance is not the primary focus, functionality is. It's also rough on the framers, but for success, it is critical that the planning and consideration that goes into designing a deck be implemented in framing. If a deck fails, it will probably be in the framing.

As you build, you need to ask if the frame is square, straight, and plumb. You also need to ask if will it resist the weather over time and remain strong for years to come. It's the job of the framer to take the time necessary to be able to answer yes to all these questions.

Deck framing ranges from the simple deck-on-grade design to very complicated decks that are elevated two or three stories off the ground. In addition, framing details vary depending on the type of decking used.

PRACTICAL CONSIDERATIONS

Before launching into framing, take the time to completely restore the project area after the footings have been installed. Remove any piles of dirt left over from excavation and smooth out any bumps or divots in the ground. Framing lumber is heavy and you don't want to be negotiating obstacles or looking for where to put your feet when trying to muscle a beam into place. If you haven't done so already, take the time to discard any demolition debris and take care of any lingering site issues, such as water supply pipes, drain lines, and electrical wiring that need to be removed or relocated. It's important to start fresh with framing.

While installing the footings for the deck, you became familiar with the site and how to move materials (as well as yourself) around efficiently. When framing, the scale increases. Before, you had to manage only a bag of concrete and a wheelbarrow; now, depending on the deck's design, you'll have to move framing lumber that can be up to 20 ft. long and weigh over 100 lb.

Flat sites present few challenges, but building on a slope is another story. Take the time to figure out how to get the lumber from the drop zone (probably the driveway) to the project zone. If there is a walkway, make sure there is enough room to navigate the longest boards around corners. If there is an existing path or you have to cut your own, consider getting a helper to move the lumber to a staging closer to the project. Moving lumber by yourself down a steep path with unsecure footing is an invitation to injury. Also, remember that framing lumber for a deck is pressure treated, so it's a good idea to wear gloves when handling it and a respirator when cutting it.

Ladders, scaffolding, and lifts

If the deck is more than just a few feet off the ground, you'll need to raise yourself as you raise the deck. Up to about 10 ft. off the ground, ladders are easy and safe to work from, although the slower the progress the higher up you go. Go higher than 10 ft., and ladders become unstable and unwieldy. Both scaffolding and lifts can be invaluable for working up high. In general, scaffolding works well for a small deck but for a larger deck where you have to move around more a lift will be more convenient, provided the terrain allows for it. For either scaffolding or a lift, you will have to reserve the rental in advance and adjust your budget to account for the extra cost.

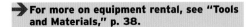

For more on equipment rental, see "Tools and Materials," p. 38.

You'll also need to weigh the cost-to-benefit ratio of renting the equipment. Sometimes, with careful planning, the deck frame itself can serve as the scaffolding. Last, the higher you go, the more helpful it is to have a crew of two or more people to lift materials, operate a cut station on the ground, and simply ferry materials up and down.

Getting help

Depending on the deck's design, it may not be practical for one person to attempt the framing. Consider the weight and length of lumber called for on the plans, the terrain, the weather, and as mentioned, the height off the ground. After accounting for all these factors, it may be safer and more cost-effective to arrange for some help for part or all of the project's framing phase.

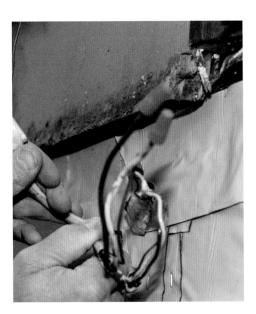

Take the time to resolve **any lingering utility issues so you can get a fresh start on the framing process and avoid costly accidents.**

WHAT CAN GO WRONG
Don't let the truck drive across the grass. Septic fields are often located under lawns and can be damaged by driving a loaded truck over them. A professional delivery driver should be aware of this, but unless you know there is no septic field there, don't risk it.

Carrying lumber down this path was actually easier than transporting the concrete bags that needed to be maneuvered in a wheelbarrow.

BEFORE YOU BEGIN

To help the job run smoothly, order your materials well in advance and have them on hand the day before you begin. Also make sure you have all the smaller items you need, like hand tools, hardware, and fasteners. A materials run can easily eat up half the morning. Make sure you have access to electrical outlets and you know where the breaker box is if you're working at someone else's home. Any details you can take care of beforehand will pay dividends if it allows you to keep the momentum of building going. Finally, check the weather. Some people don't mind working in inclement weather but to attach the ledger board onto a remodel, you might have to remove the siding. If the forecast calls for rain, either hold off for better weather or rig up a tarp.

TRADE SECRET
Get it delivered the way you want it. When ordering lumber, specify how you want the wood stacked. Put the posts on top, then the beams, and then the ledger and joist material. That way, as you use the materials you don't have to shuffle items in the stack.

LEDGER BASICS

For most decks, framing begins with locating and installing the ledger. As discussed in the design chapter, ledgers are critical components of a deck because they support a substantial amount of the deck's load. If not detailed correctly, they are the gateway for water entering the house.

Most deck failures occur where the ledger ties into the house. Either the connection between the house and the ledger was inadequate or the ledger allowed water to infiltrate the frame of the house, causing rot and ultimately the deck's failure. Usually the deck ledger is located in reference to a door providing access to the house. In areas that are prone to heavy winter snow accumulation, the main deck elevation is located one or even two steps below the doorsill to prevent windblown snow from piling up against the door.

➡ **See also "Why Not Just Skip The Ledger?," p. 20.**

In this section, we'll cover standard ledger installation techniques for both remodel and new construction. For remodel, we will outline adding a new ledger to a wall with existing siding. We'll also talk about flashing for both new construction and extreme environments. You'll learn how to locate the height of the ledger, install flashing, attach the ledger, and finally how to secure the ledger with code-compliant hardware.

What you'll need

Here's a list of the items that are essential for deck framing. For more detailed information, see "Tools and Materials" on p. 38.

- 4×4 or 4×6 posts
- 2×8 or 2×10 ledger and joist stock
- Ledger attachment hardware
- Joist hangers
- Post-to-joist attachment hardware
- Corrosion-resistant fasteners
- Circular saw
- Hammer
- Chalkline
- Measuring tape
- Square
- Awl
- Drill/driver
- Self-leveling rotary laser (can be rented)
- Safety protection for your eyes, ears, and lungs

Attaching the ledger is the culmination of much preparation.

ESTABLISHING A CONTROL LINE

1 Position the laser where the beam can register all the places to be marked.

2 Turn on the level and make sure it broadcasts its beam correctly.

3 Consistently mark the center of the projected light beam. Even though it is called a laser, the beam of light is not that precise.

4 Make a series of marks to identify the control line that you will use as a reference when flashing and installing the ledger.

A control line is a level reference line (or a series of marks) used to establish the elevations of the different deck components. Use a laser lever to establish the line below or above any of the deck details so that nothing interferes with the line as you proceed **1,2**. As when building the foundation, it's worth renting or buying a quality laser level. Spirit levels are not accurate over distances of more than 10 ft.

When using the laser, mark the center of the laser indicator to ensure accuracy **3**. The farther the laser level is from the wall the fatter the line will get, so referencing off the top or bottom will not be consistent. It's also important to remember that the control line is not a line. It's actually a series of marks at key locations along an imaginary line **4**. There are two reasons to use a laser level to establish the control line rather than snapping a chalkline. First, the chalkline will have to be cleaned up at the end of the job, and second, a horizontal chalkline snapped over 8 ft. might sag. Key locations for marking the control line are under each door jamb, at the building corners, and at a couple of intervals along the run. We have an 8-ft. level, so we like to mark the control line every 8 ft. or so.

LOCATING THE LEDGER ELEVATION

1 Place a level under the door threshold to determine the lowest point. Use this as a reference to establish the elevation of the finished deck.

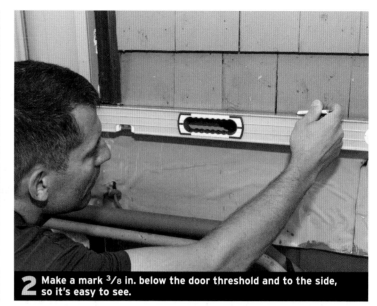

2 Make a mark 3/8 in. below the door threshold and to the side, so it's easy to see.

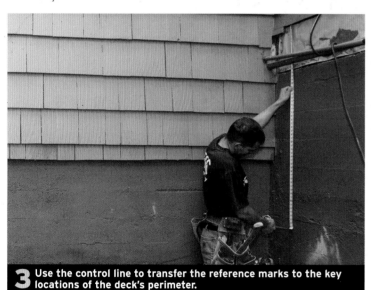

3 Use the control line to transfer the reference marks to the key locations of the deck's perimeter.

4 Cut the siding with a circular saw, typically 3/8 in. above the finished deck elevation.

If the main access door to the deck already exists, locating the deck ledger's elevation, or height, is straightforward. Use 3/8 in. below the bottom of the door threshold as the finished deck height **1**. The 3/8-in. gap will allow water to drain away and account for any construction vagaries down the line. If the threshold is slightly out of level, use the lower side to reference the deck elevation **2**. If the door is seriously out of level, you may want to consider resetting the door. Measure the distance to the control line and subtract the thickness of the decking. This is the distance from the control line to the top of the framing. At the key locations, measure up that distance and mark the top of the ledger **3**. Now measure up from that line the thickness of the decking plus the 3/8-in. gap and make a mark. This establishes the siding termination above the deck (see "A Control Line Is the Reference for All the Deck's Elevations" on p. 94).

Determining where to cut the siding will depend on what the finish siding will look like and what flashing details are required. For the project shown here, the siding terminates at the height of the door threshold. In some marine environments or areas prone to rot, you might consider terminating the siding 1 in. or 2 in. above the decking and bridging the gap with metal flashing. Finally, strike the line of siding termination and cut this with a circular saw **4**.

➤ See also "Flashing a ledger for extreme weather exposure," p. 104.

LOCATING THE LEDGER ELEVATION (CONTINUED)

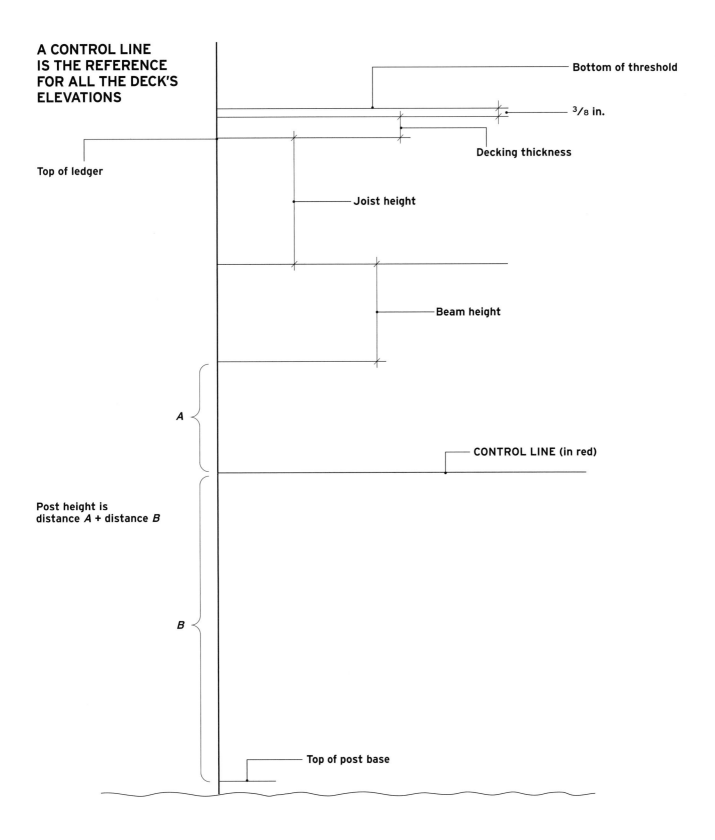

A CONTROL LINE
IS THE REFERENCE
FOR ALL THE DECK'S
ELEVATIONS

Bottom of threshold

$^3/_8$ in.

Decking thickness

Top of ledger

Joist height

Beam height

CONTROL LINE (in red)

Post height is
distance A + distance B

A

B

Top of post base

1 Reference the control line to establish the ledger location. First, mark the ledger elevation without the drop.

2 Measure down the calculated drop, 1/16 in. per foot of run.

3 Draw and label all the decking elements right on the existing siding. Double-check your measurements.

4 Snap chalklines where you want to cut away the siding. Never snap lines where you don't intend to make a cut.

Accounting for ledger slope

A deck needs to drop in elevation 1/16 in. per foot of run to ensure that water on the deck flows away from the house. Typically, the drop runs away from the main part of the house and perpendicular to the decking. The deck shown here connected to the house on two sides, which meant we had to account for the drop when locating the side ledger. Besides adding the drop, the steps for installing this side ledger are also the steps for installing a ledger for a deck addition.

To locate a ledger, measure up from the control line and mark the established top-of-ledger elevation at both ends **1**. Then, at the end where you want the drop, measure down 1/16 in. per foot of run and mark the new top of the ledger **2**.

From the new top of the ledger, measure the height of the ledger plus 3/8 in., to allow for variations in the lumber size, and mark the cutline for the bottom of the ledger. To avoid confusion, mark and label the elements of framing, decking, and gap directly on the siding **3**. If you are not going to paint, try to keep your labels inside the perimeter so they won't be visible after the siding is cut back. Drawing the layout directly on the siding is an extra step, but it's important to double-check your layout before cutting the siding. We've found that having the actual layout visible can prevent the very costly mistake of mis-cutting the siding. Once you're sure everything is correct, snap chalklines only where you need to cut **4**.

REMOVING SIDING

On this project, the siding was cedar sidewall shingles, which are easy to cut with a circular saw. However, depending on the project details, you may encounter siding materials such as fiber cement, vinyl, composite, metal, or some combination of these. It is beyond the scope of this book to address all the situations you might encounter, but, in general, use the cutting tool and blade specified by the siding manufacturer. In some situations you may have to remove a section of siding to cut it effectively and then reinstall it.

If you're cutting wood or wood composite, a circular saw will work most of the time. Plunge-cutting with a circular saw is the easiest way to begin the cut ❶. When removing shingles, it is easy to make the top and bottom cuts and remove the shingles in that section before moving the ladder to a new location. If the cladding is lap siding or a panel product, cut the entire top line first and remove any loose siding or pieces held in place only by paint ❷. Then cut the bottom line ❸, remove all the siding in between, and strip the section down to bare sheathing ❹. It can be challenging to remove the siding in inside corners and around utilities. Note that an oscillating cutter can be extremely helpful at making cuts in tight spots ❺. Once the siding and building paper have been removed, clean up the stripped section and repair and secure any areas of the sheathing ❻.

1 Begin the cut slightly in from the end and take the line as you cut.

2 Remove the siding freed by the top cut. Using a smaller tool here will reduce the chance of damaging siding not slated for removal.

3 Cut the line along the ledger's bottom using the same technique as for the top line.

4 Remove all the siding, nails, and other debris behind where the ledger will be attached.

5 Complete the siding removal by cutting out the siding and building paper in the corners using an oscillating tool.

6 Repair or reattach any damaged or loose pieces of sheathing material.

WHAT CAN GO WRONG

It's common to find rot behind siding. This is especially true if your deck project includes removing an existing deck ledger. It's critical to find the source of the rot and fix it before proceeding. This may involve removing more siding, replacing sheathing, or even hiring a contractor to deal with the specific issue. Whatever you do, don't let the rot go unaddressed.

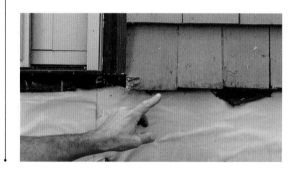

TRADE SECRET

To determine the blade depth of a blind cut like this, first measure the siding thickness at the bottom of the siding (top, below). Cut a short distance along the cut line and remove the siding to check the depth of the cut (bottom, below), and then adjust the blade depth accordingly.

INSTALLING LEDGER FLASHING

1 Cut any fasteners hidden behind the siding above the ledger location. A side grinder fitted with a thin abrasive blade works well for this task.

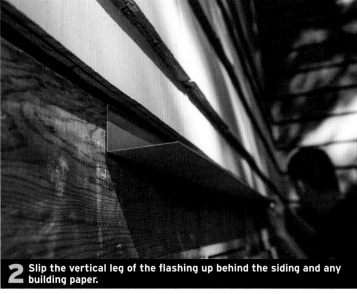

2 Slip the vertical leg of the flashing up behind the siding and any building paper.

3 At flashing joints, overlap the flashing pieces by a healthy amount to prevent water infiltration.

4 Caulk any flashing joints where water can penetrate. Here, a daub of caulk was applied between the layers of flashing.

Different conditions call for different ledger flashing details. The flashing details in regions that experience extreme weather, especially wind-driven rain, will be different from those in drier regions, like the desert, where wood takes much longer to rot and metals take tens of decades to corrode. In the following pages, we present several options for installing flashing, which will guide you to the best details for your local conditions.

Flashing a ledger for a remodel

Installing ledger flashing for a remodel where the existing siding is in place is different from installing ledger flashing where no siding is installed. If the project is vulnerable to extreme weather, you need to consider removing enough siding to flash the ledger more thoroughly. When the siding is already installed, the goal is to flash as thoroughly as possible but to disturb as little of the siding

as possible. To do this, use a combination of metal flashing, self-adhesive flashing, and building paper.

➡ See "Flashing a ledger for new construction," p. 101.

➡ See "Flashing a ledger for extreme weather exposure," p. 104.

5 Install Z-flashing where the siding is cut away under the ledger. This will direct any water behind the ledger to the outside.

6 Tape the Z-flashing in place with small squares of flashing tape to secure it for the next step.

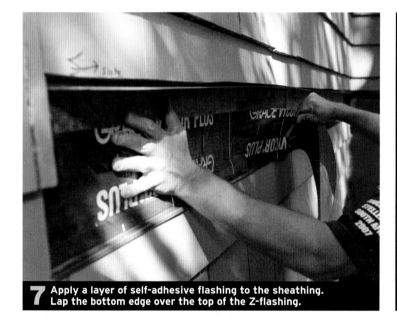

7 Apply a layer of self-adhesive flashing to the sheathing. Lap the bottom edge over the top of the Z-flashing.

8 Rub the self-adhesive flashing where it contacts the Z-flashing to ensure a good seal.

Before installing any flashing, free the siding above the ledger from any hidden fasteners **1**. This allows the vertical leg of the L-flashing to slip up behind both the existing siding and the building paper **2**. If the ledger is longer than a length of flashing, overlap the pieces by at least 8 in. to 10 in. to prevent water from running along the flashing and behind the ledger **3**. There is no need to caulk this joint; however, in an inside

corner where the flashing overlap is only 2 in., it's a good idea to apply a daub of caulk between the overlap to prevent water from seeping into the corner **4**.

At the bottom of the ledger opening, install Z-flashing to direct any water that gets behind the ledger out and over the siding **5**. Note that Z-flashing can be hard to work with, especially on a windy day. If you're having difficulty controlling the

flashing, use small squares of tape to hold it in place **6**. Protect the sheathing against water infiltration at the fasteners with a layer of self-adhesive flashing **7**. The flashing does not need to extend all the way to the top of the opening, but take care to fully adhere the adhesive flashing membrane to the Z-flashing's vertical section **8**. The stand on this leg is typically too short to depend on gravity to keep the water out.

INSTALLING LEDGER FLASHING (CONTINUED)

9 Install a layer of felt building paper lapped over the adhesive flashing and under the L-flashing above.

Use a layer of felt building paper over the flashing to help direct any water that gets behind the siding above the deck to the outside **9**. Installation can be a little tricky but try to slip the building paper as far up behind the L-flashing as possible.

The spot where the siding meets the end of the ledger is very vulnerable to both water infiltration and rot. To help protect this area, slide a piece of flat metal flashing behind the adjacent siding **10**. Then, before installing the ledger, apply a thick bead of caulk in the corner and install the ledger before the caulk cures **11**. This method of flashing penetration is not foolproof. Further, it is probably insufficient for places like Nova Scotia and overkill for an environment like Death Valley. If your project will be exposed to high winds or abnormally high drainage due to the overall house design, then consider removing enough siding to flash 8 in. to 10 in. out from the ledger perimeter (see "Additional Protection for Wet Climates" on p. 103).

11 Apply a thick bead of caulk where the flashing meets the siding just before installing the ledger board.

10 Insert metal flashing behind the siding at either end of the ledger to protect the siding and sheathing at this vulnerable spot.

TRADE SECRET

While the sheathing is still exposed, lightly mark the wall stud locations on the siding either above or below the opening so you can locate the studs easily when securing the ledger.

Flashing a ledger for new construction

In situations where you can install the ledger before the siding (typical of new construction and additions), the flashing can be installed to more thoroughly protect the ledger-to-house connection from water infiltration and rot. To begin, find the ledger location by using the control-line method described earlier in this chapter.

➡ See "Establishing a Control Line," p. 92.

Begin by fastening a piece of metal Z-flashing at the bottom of the ledger location and then cut the building paper at the top of the flashing ❶. To adequately flash at the end of the ledger, cut the building paper at a 45° angle starting at the end of the Z-flashing ❷. This cut should extend about 6 in. above the top of the ledger location.

Once both ends are cut, fold the building paper up and temporarily hold it out of the way with some tape ❸. As when installing flashing for a remodel, prevent water infiltration through the fastener holes used to secure the ledger by applying a layer of self-adhesive flashing against the sheathing behind the membrane ❹. Extend the flashing well beyond the end of the ledger and position it so it fully laps over the Z-flashing's

1 Cut the building paper with a utility knife, using the top of the Z-metal flashing as a guide for the blade.

2 Mark and make a secondary cut at 45°, running away from the ledger's end at the bottom.

3 Temporarily tape the building paper out of the way. Use green or blue tape for this, not pieces of the self-adhesive flashing.

4 Apply a continuous piece of self-adhesive flashing behind the ledger to seal the ledger fasteners.

INSTALLING LEDGER FLASHING (CONTINUED)

5 Lap the self-adhesive flashing over the Z-flashing so it fully covers the Z-flashing's horizontal leg.

6 Rub the flashing to make sure it fully adheres to the wall sheathing.

7 Seat the ledger against the Z-flashing and install it using the appropriate fasteners and schedule.

8 Install 3-in. L-flashing seated against the ledger top and secured with galvanized staples or nails.

edge **5**. Sometimes, especially in cold weather and depending on the brand, you will need to rub the flashing to make sure it adheres to the sheathing. You can buy a roller made for this purpose, but we find that we can use a Speed Square as long as we're careful not to damage the membrane **6**.

At this point, position the ledger with the end flush to the Z-flashing and attach it with the appropriate fasteners **7**.

➤ See "Installing the Ledger," p. 106.

Once the ledger is secured, apply 3 in. of L-flashing over the top to direct water away from the ledger **8**. We use a ⅛-in. pneumatic crown stapler for this, but you can also secure the flashing with small galvanized nails or stainless-steel screws. Try to secure the flashing as high up on the leg as possible. Let the flashing overhang

the end of the ledger by 2 in. to cover the end joist and protect the fasteners that secure it to the ledger **9**. If there is a gap between the top of the diagonal cut in the building paper and the top of the self-adhesive membrane, cover it with a square of membrane before folding the building paper down **10**. The siding will eventually lap over the building paper. However, you can cut the paper now in the correct place by putting a spacer equal to the decking thickness on the flashing and using that as a guide for cutting the building paper with a utility knife **11**. Finally, apply tape to seal the area. Like all cladding, the tape gets applied from the bottom first so the upper pieces lap over the lower pieces **12**.

TRADE SECRET

The adhesive used on some brands of self-adhesive flashing can be very tacky and extremely difficult to reposition if placed in the wrong location by mistake. Here is an installation trick to avoid a sticky mess: With the backing still in place, position the flashing where it will be installed and mark the perimeter. Once the perimeter is marked, peel the backing and apply the membrane in the perfect position in one try.

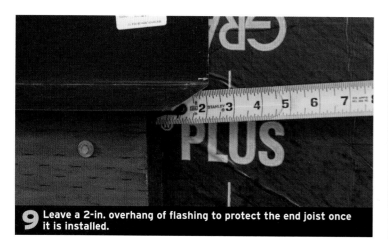

9 Leave a 2-in. overhang of flashing to protect the end joist once it is installed.

10 Flash any overcut of the building paper to prevent water infiltration.

11 Cut the housewrap to the height of the finished deck, using a scrap of decking as a guide block.

12 Trim any excess building paper and seal the seams with tape.

ADDITIONAL PROTECTION FOR WET CLIMATES

In some wet climates, it's a good idea to protect aluminum flashing from the corrosive effects of pressure-treated lumber by separating them with a membrane. How much protection you need to install to prevent water infiltration and rot depends on your climate. What could be considered adequate in areas of the Southwest would be severely negligent in the Northeast.

INSTALLING LEDGER FLASHING (CONTINUED)

Flashing a ledger for extreme weather exposure

In areas that experience extreme weather conditions, such as high humidity, frequent rains, windblown rain, or heavy snowfall, the deck will need extra protection, especially in the ledger area. The following steps will help provide additional protection to the ledger to prevent rot and corrosion.

After securing the ledger, add a layer of self-adhesive flashing over the ledger board to protect it from water infiltration and to protect the hardware from corrosive preservative chemicals ❶. Wrap this membrane from the bottom, where the ledger meets the Z-flashing, all the way to the top of the ledger and up the wall by at least 2 in. ❷. If it is not fully seated into the inside corner, the metal L-flashing will not sit against the wall. For this application, use stainless-steel L-flashing with 3-in. legs on top of the ledger rather than galvanized L-flashing ❸. For extreme weather scenarios, galvanized, and even copper, flashing may corrode over time if left in direct contact with the chemicals used in pressure-treated lumber. As a result, stainless steel is the best choice.

Use a spacer to mark the deck height on the flashing ❹. Obviously, a piece of decking is good for this, but if you don't have any decking on hand yet, you can use a scrap of wood. Lap another 6-in. section of self-adhesive flashing over the stainless-steel flashing, flush to the line you just made, to prevent windblown moisture from infiltrating above the flashing's vertical leg ❺. Finally, fold the building paper down and trim it flush with the bottom of the self-adhesive flashing ❻.

1 Apply a layer of self-adhesive flashing over the ledger board to protect the ledger and the hardware.

2 Use your finger to fully seat the membrane in the corner at the ledger's top.

TRADE SECRET

Using self-adhesive flashing can be tricky because it sticks to everything, especially itself. The difficulty increases exponentially as the width of the flashing increases and the ambient temperature rises. There is help, though. Inserted under the backing paper of the tape is a release cord. Pulling this cord out cuts the backing paper in half, which enables you to expose only half of the adhesive surface at a time. Once the upper half of the tape is set, remove the backing on the lower half and press the flashing into place. However, finding the cord can be a challenge in itself.

3 Secure 3-in. stainless-steel L-flashing with ⅛-in. staples or small nails.

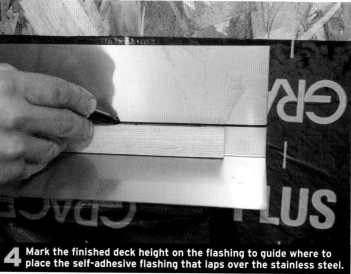

4 Mark the finished deck height on the flashing to guide where to place the self-adhesive flashing that laps over the stainless steel.

5 Apply a layer of 6-in. self-adhesive flashing over the L-flashing.

6 Lap the building paper over the flashing assembly and tape any seams as necessary.

ALTERNATIVE METHOD FOR EXTREME FLASHING

An alternative to fully encasing the ledger in self-adhesive membrane is to protect against hardware corrosion only at the location where the hardware touches the membrane. The advantage of this method is that it saves time and money. The disadvantage is that in some extreme environments, the ledger can still become water soaked, and if the water contacts the fasteners inside the wood, they could begin to corrode.

INSTALLING THE LEDGER

1 Measure the siding cutback to establish the ledger length.

2 Check the crown to save yourself from fighting with a severely crowned board.

3 Cut the ledger from pressure-treated joist stock. Remember to account for a 1/8-in. gap at either end.

4 Seal the fresh cut with wood preservative and allow to dry for a minute or so.

Installing the ledger is the final step in establishing the deck elevation, so it's worth taking the extra time to locate the ledger precisely before permanently securing it. First, double-check the siding cutback to establish the length of the ledger. If you're working alone, pick a spot in the middle and measure the distance on both sides and then add them up **1**. Before cutting the ledger, sight down the board and identify and mark the crown **2**. If the crown is greater than 1/2 in., select a different board as the ledger. Subtract 1/4 in. from the length for 1/8 in. of

wiggle room on either end **3**. As with all freshly cut ends, protect the ledger with wood preservative **4**.

If you are working alone, this is a good time to pause and ask yourself if you need some help. If the ledger installation is more than a few feet off the ground, if the footing is precarious, or if the ledger is over 10 ft. long, get some help to hold the ledger in place while it's temporarily secured **5**. Use 3-in. screws to temporarily hold the ledger in place until it can be fastened permanently **6**. This allows you to use the control line to double-check

the ledger location **7**. Make sure to seat the flashing against the ledger's top. There should be at least a 1 1/8-in. gap between the flashing and siding to prevent standing water from wicking up behind the siding.

Each project will have different requirements for permanently securing the ledger. For this job, we were able to run 5/8-in. lag screws into the wall studs behind the sheathing for adequate attachment.

5 Place the ledger in position, resting it on the flashing until it is secured.

7 Measure up from the control line and adjust the ledger to its final position.

6 Drive one 3-in. screw at either end to temporarily secure the ledger while adjusting the position.

LEDGER ATTACHMENT HARDWARE

Different scenarios require different hardware. The two main categories of ledger fasteners are lag screws and through bolts. Lag screws bite with threads into solid framing members like studs or beams. Conversely, as the name implies, through bolts are passed through a framing member, typically a rim joist, and secured with a bolt. Often the framing member inside the house that you are attaching the ledger to will need further reinforcement.

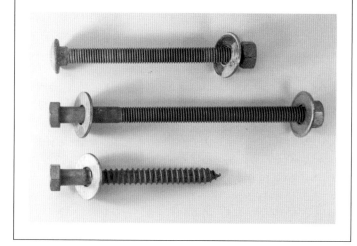

INSTALLING THE LEDGER (CONTINUED)

Marking the ledger

Mark the wall-stud location on the ledger's face. You can find the locations by pulling the layout from one known stud location or by marking the stud locations before installing the ledger ❶.

Drive fasteners through the ledger and into the wall stud at every stud location. As shown, a FastenMaster Ledger Lok lag bolt does not require a pilot hole ❷.

Locate fasteners 2 in. from the top and bottom edges of the ledger board. This reduces the chance the ledger will split due to applied load (and it's a code requirement in most areas) ❸.

Install fasteners at every stud location. Decks designed by an architect may call for a specific fastener pattern but otherwise assume two fasteners at every stud location ❹.

DETERMINING POST HEIGHT

Posts and beams are the substructure elements of the deck that take the diffuse load of the joists, decking, and everything on top of the decking and direct it to the footings in the ground. The difficulty of installing these framing members is that there is nothing to support them. As a result, much of the work of setting posts and beams is bracing them securely during the installation process.

Posts and beams are generally installed from the ground up. While this may sound self-evident because the beams rest on the posts, there are situations, especially on uneven terrain, where it's easier to install a beam, attached at the ends, and then install the posts that support the beam between the corners. In this section, you'll learn both methods as well as common bracing strategies and tips for installing hardware.

We used the laser level when installing the ledger, but this tool really earns its place on the job when determining post height. If possible, position the laser so the laser line matches the control line you used to install the ledger. If you can't do this, establish a new control line. The deck shown here has a common framing scenario, where a girder beam supports the joists from underneath and the post height is to the bottom of that beam.

→ **See also "Selecting Post Sizes," p. 21.**

To determine post height, you need to add two measurements together. First, take the distance from the bottom of the ledger to the control line and subtract the beam height ❶. Write this first measurement down and use it as the top portion of every post. The second portion is from the center of the post base up to the laser line ❷. It will quickly become apparent why the laser level is so valuable because it is very difficult to accurately and quickly achieve this second measurement for each post base without a laser. For each post base, repeat the process of adding the constant top measurement to the individual post's second measurement.

❶ Measure down from the bottom of the ledger to the control line and subtract the height of the beam.

❷ Place the end of the tape on the post base and measure up to the laser line to get the second measurement.

TRADE SECRET

Avoid confusion by writing the post height on the post-base hardware. Writing all the post heights down on a piece of paper—or worse, a scrap of wood—will just lead to frustration when you lose it. Instead keep the post height handy by writing it where you will need it, on the post base.

SETTING AND BRACING POSTS

The framing process would move a lot faster if nothing had to be braced. Unfortunately, even a post base that will hold a beam upright on its own won't hold the post securely without a brace. Decide on a bracing scheme before setting the post. This will save you time and materials because you can avoid redundant bracing—or worse, incomplete bracing that may allow the framing to fall down during construction.

For this deck, we chose to cross-brace the two end posts with an additional tie to the house and brace laterally to the posts between the ends. Before cutting the first post, we like to mark all the elevations on the post and then double-check the actual measurements against the ledger already installed ❶. This may seem like an unnecessary step, but it takes only an extra minute and eliminates the possibility of a math error. Likewise, take the time to mark the cutline all around the post rather than on just one side ❷. When framing, a series of small errors in accuracy can compound to

---

BRACING FRAMING TEMPORARILY

Shown here are three common bracing strategies, depending on the specifics of your job. If the house provides a good reference but you can't securely attach the beam to it, cross-bracing can hold posts (Method 1). When the beam can be secured to the house, the combination of fixed post bases and the beam stabilizes the structure and no cross-bracing is required (Method 2). At times the deck framing cannot be tied to the house at all, and in those scenarios cross-bracing is the best choice and may have to be permanent (Method 3).

To temporarily brace a run of posts laterally, use stakes to secure the posts at the ground and then screw them to the posts halfway up.

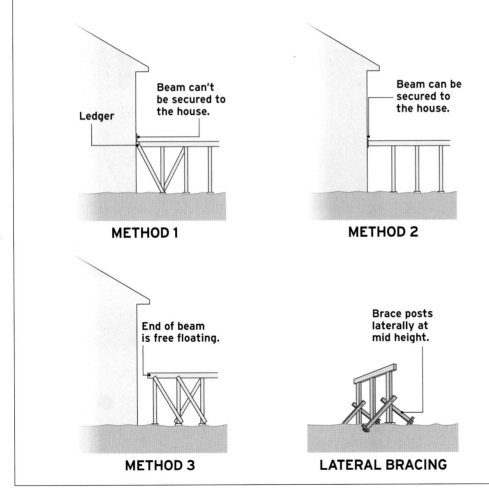

METHOD 1
Ledger
Beam can't be secured to the house.

METHOD 2
Beam can be secured to the house.

METHOD 3
End of beam is free floating.

LATERAL BRACING
Brace posts laterally at mid height.

WHAT CAN GO WRONG
Take the time to set aside any warped, twisted, or bowed stock even if it means another trip to the lumberyard. Pressure-treated lumber can be of questionable quality, so if you didn't select the lumber yourself, plan on finding a few posts that are better for modern sculpture than for structural support.

Bracing is required to keep everything aligned until the posts are permanently secured.

1 Mark all the important elevations on one post to use as a story pole before making any cuts.

2 Clearly mark the cutline on at least two sides to help guide your cuts.

SETTING AND BRACING POSTS (CONTINUED)

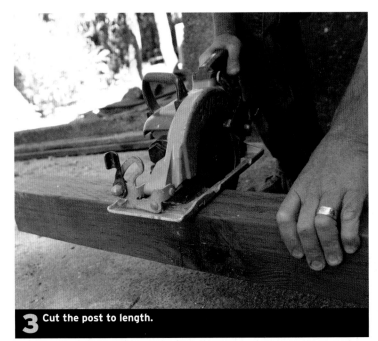

3 Cut the post to length.

4 Secure the post in the base with 1½-in. hanger nails, being sure to use every hole.

5 Brace the posts as you install them rather than bracing them all at once after installation.

6 Screw the brace to the ledger to add stability.

make the final product noticeably out of level or out of square. Tracing the line all around the post saves time when cutting because you can flip the beam to make the second cut on the opposite side instead of running around it with the blade while cutting the adjacent side **3**.

Once the post is cut, you need to apply wood preservative. Use a brush or pour a small amount into a bucket and dip the cut end into the preservative. Position the post onto the base and fill every hole with a hanger nail to secure the post to the base **4**. In some cases, the plans may call

for a bolt installation to connect the post and base for protection against wind uplift.

When you have two posts installed, brace the posts according to your bracing scheme **5**. Run the brace long so you can secure it to the ledger with a toe screw **6**. Generally, although posts are secured to the

7 Secure the tops of the posts with lateral bracing as well as attachment to the post base.

8 Install perpendicular bracing in both directions to temporarily hold the bracing until the beams and joists are installed.

9 Fold a square of self-adhesive flashing over the top end of the post to protect it from rot and the post hardware from corrosion.

bases with galvanized nails, all the bracing is secured with star-headed screws. Screws are easier to remove than nails, and the star-headed screws won't strip as easily as Phillips®-head screws.

➜ **See also "Framing hardware and fasteners," p. 58.**

Once the bracing is anchored, by either a section of cross braces or a leg that is tied into a stable structure, additional posts can be adequately secured with lateral bracing at the top **7**. As long as the cross brace on the first post remains secure, the rest of the posts will remain in place. After a run of posts is in place, plumb and brace each

post perpendicular to the beam direction **8**. These braces can be shorter, bracing the post in the center as opposed to the top. The last step when setting posts is to protect the top of the beam from water and rot **9**. This will also help minimize hardware corrosion.

SETTING AND BRACING POSTS (CONTINUED)

Setting posts from the top down

When a beam spans between two points of the deck that are already installed, it is easier to put the beam in place and cut the posts to length rather than trying to use a control line to determine the post length.

Once you've set the beam in place, run a string along one edge and check the beam for straightness ❶. If the beam has a bow or sag to it, correct it before measuring for post height. If you don't, you'll build this flaw into the deck. You may have to prop the beam up or weigh it down accordingly.

➤ See "Installing Beams," p. 117.

To install a post under the beam, you'll first need to position the post-base hard-ware and then mark the post length. To position the hardware, place the post on the footing with the top against the beam plumb in both directions ❷. When plumb, the post is adjacent to where it will be installed. Use the edges to mark the final location on the underside of the beam ❸. Before moving the post, mark the correct location on the footing as well ❹. Use the post to mark one side and a scrap of wood aligned with the side of the post to mark a second side of the final post location. In theory, you could use the marks to find the center of the post base by simply align-ing the base to the marks. However, this is slightly inaccurate and a more precise method is to use a plumb bob ❺. Finally, place the post-base hardware on the foot-ing ❻. The edges and bolt hole should all align with the marks you just made. Now install the hardware per the manufacturer's instructions.

➤ See "Installing Footing Hardware," p. 80.

Once the post base is installed, determine the post length by placing the post's edge on the base and holding it to the marks you made on the beam's underside ❼. Cut the post to length and treat the bottom end with wood preservative and cap the top with self-adhesive flashing. In an ideal world the post will slip into place with a slight upward lift to the beam ❽.

1 Check the beam for straightness by stretching a string along one edge and sighting along the beam and string.

2 Plumb a post (not cut to length) adjacent to the final install location.

3 Mark the post center and edges on the underside of the beam.

4 Mark two sides of the post location on the base using one side of the post and a scrap of wood set at a right angle.

5 Mark the post center on the footing with a plumb bob aligned with the post's centerline marked on the beam.

6 Use the marks to align the post base on the concrete footing.

7 Mark the post to length by positioning it as plumb as possible in the post base.

8 Slip the post into place and temporarily secure it with a screw until the final hardware is installed.

TRADE SECRET

Don't assume that the beam dimensions are consistent. Lumber dimensions can vary by as much as $1/4$ in. or more, especially with pressure-treated wood. Take the time to measure the actual size of your beam before making any calculations of post height.

SETTING AND BRACING POSTS (CONTINUED)

TRADE SECRET

If the beam has a sag to it, you might be tempted to prop it up with a 2×4 cut to length, but there's a better way. To prop up a beam without cutting lumber, simply drive a nail into the side and use that to lift the beam. The nail won't hold a lot of weight but it will hold enough to lift the beam ¼ in., which can be enough to allow you to slip the post into place without having to fight with it.

WHAT CAN GO WRONG

Don't trust the factory to make perfect cuts. Sometimes the factory cuts look as if they were made by a blind chimp wielding a chainsaw. If the cut is off, take the time to square it up and give it a coat of wood preservative.

INSTALLING BEAMS

If you are going to call on a friend to help build a deck, there is no better time to do it than when setting the beams. To be able to support the joists and decking, beams are necessarily big, heavy, and hard to move into place. Whether you are working with a helper or alone, double-check the post locations and bracing before tackling beams: Standing on a ladder with the beam on your shoulder is not the time to realize a post is in the wrong spot or cut to the wrong height. Also, take the time to work out a plan for

how you will lift the beam; be realistic. Slipping a disc in your back will slow down the project more than taking the time to get enough hands on a beam to safely lift it into place.

➡ See "Moving lumber alone," p. 36.

On the deck shown here, we decided to use two 10-ft. beams spliced in the middle rather than a 20-ft. beam, which would have been more expensive, required special delivery, and been harder to manage on the job

site ❶. To set a beam, measure the beam's length centered on the post you will split the beam on. Later you will add some hardware to beef up this connection. Because there is minimal bearing on a 4×4 post, take the time to make perfectly square cuts where the beams meet. Clearly mark the cut line on all four sides of the beam ❷. If the saw is out of square, you will know it after one cut and can make a correction for the second cut ❸. Because the blade on a typical circular saw will not clear the beam, there is no

1 Measure the length of the beam from the end to the center of the post you want to split the beam over.

2 Mark the cutline on all four sides of the beam to ensure the squarest cut possible.

3 Place the beam in a stable location to make the cut, then make two passes, one from each face, with a circular saw.

TRADE SECRET

Mind the gap! A beam will often have a slight crown. Before toe-screwing the beam to the post at the midspan or installing hardware, seat the beam to the post. An easy, low-tech way to do this is to sit on it while driving in the screw.

INSTALLING BEAMS (CONTINUED)

4 Apply a wood preservative to protect the end of the beam against rot and insect damage.

5 Lift one end of the beam and rest it securely close to its final position.

6 Lift the other end of the beam and rest it on top of the post.

7 Shift the beam until it bears on half the post.

need to sticker the lumber off the ground. However, before applying the wood preservative, block the beam's end off the ground and place a scrap under it so excess preservative does not contaminate the soil **4**.

If you are lifting the beam alone, raise one end into place and make sure it is secure **5**. Here, we were able to use some of the bracing to hold the beam in place. With one end secure, lift the other end into place **6**. This method allows you to raise the beam into position while having to support only half of the weight at any given moment. Position the beam to split on the post **7** and toe-screw the end to the post to secure it temporarily **8**. Once the abutting beam is in place, toe-screw it to the first beam instead of the post **9**. The screws are needed only until the connecting hardware gets installed.

8 Drive a screw, toed at an angle, to temporarily secure the beam.

9 Follow the same procedure to lift the adjoining beam and secure it with a screw.

TRADE SECRET

Cutting a 4-in. by 6-in. beam with a typical circular saw requires two deep passes. To make a good cut, the sawblade needs to be dead-on-square to the saw foot, so it's a good habit to check the blade for square before making the cut. Remember to unplug the saw when checking.

TRADE SECRET

When assembling framing, we prefer to use screws rather than nails for two reasons. First, after you've taken the time to carefully position a beam, it's too easy to knock it out of alignment while nailing. Second, if you find you want to reposition the beam, it's much easier to back out a screw than to pull a galvanized nail.

INSTALLING BEAMS (CONTINUED)

— INSTALLING POST CAPS —

Complete the framing assembly before installing the post-to-beam hardware. This will save time during construction and allow you to easily make corrections where necessary ❶.

Position the post-to-beam hardware snug against the framing materials and drive a galvanized fastener through the lower flange to secure it to the post ❷.

Install one side of the two-part unity, filling every hole with a fastener. Then move on to the other side ❸.

Secure the joint between two beams adding a mending plate above the post-cap flange. I tack the plate on either side level and then drive the rest of the fasteners ❹.

Fill every fastener hole. There is a tendency not to fill every hole since there are so many but the engineered plate rating is based on all the fasteners being installed ❺.

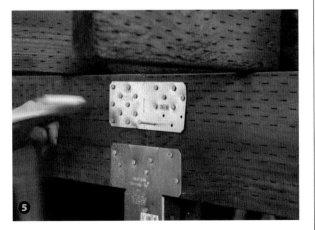

PULLING LAYOUT

Once the beams are installed and either temporarily or permanently braced, it's time to install the joists. Installing the joists involves pulling an initial layout of their locations and marking the house ledger, rolling the lumber into place, and installing rim joists. However, these tasks are not discrete. Often there will be a little back and forth among them. For example, it's easier to register secondary layouts off of joists that have already been installed rather than doing the entire layout before installing any joists.

In this section, we'll discuss how to pull an initial layout and square the assembly. Then you'll learn different ways to pull secondary layouts, some of which involve joists that have already been installed. We'll cover installing, or rolling, joists in the next section.

Most commonly, joist spacing is 16 in. o.c., but it can vary depending on the type of decking. Some synthetic decking requires joist spacing at 12 in.; and if the deck is going to carry a heavy load, such as a hot tub, the joist spacing will often be reduced even more. For the deck shown here, we used standard 16-in.-o.c. joist spacing.

The easiest way to pull layout is simply to hook the tape on the end of the ledger board and mark a crow's foot every 16 in. **❶**. On this deck, we wanted the layout to begin from the outside of the rim joist that hadn't been installed yet. We could have stopped what we were doing to install the rim joist before pulling layout, but instead we dropped (or burned) 1¹⁄₂ in. from the layout so that every joist was 16-in. o.c. **❷**. When marking the joist location, indicate with an X which side of the crow's foot to locate the joist **❸** (p. 122). It's also a good idea to draw a vertical line to indicate the edge of the joist **❹** (p. 122). This makes it easy to install the joist by aligning the joist face to the line.

Install the rim joist to the end of the ledger with through screws **❺** (p. 122). There are a couple of things to note about installing the rim joist. First, as mentioned, you can install the rim joist before pulling layout and simply hook your tape to it instead of

1 Hook the tape measure on the end of the ledger board and mark each joist on the layout.

2 Adjust the layout so that all the joists are aligned on center in reference to the end joist.

burning 1¹⁄₂ in. to get all the joists 16 in. o.c. Second, installing the rim joist to the end of the ledger, as seen here, has the advantage that it can be secured with through screws instead of hardware. If the rim joist butts to a full-length ledger, then corner-attachment hardware is required **❻** (p. 122). Once the rim joist is secured to the ledger, use the 3-4-5 method to align it at 90° to the house.

➜ **See "Squaring with the 3-4-5 Method,"** p. 72.

PULLING LAYOUT (CONTINUED)

3 Mark the side of the crow's foot that the joist will land on to avoid any confusion.

4 Mark a plumb line to align the joist to when installing the joists.

─ WHERE TO START JOIST LAYOUT ─

Start the layout from the logical spot, which is not necessarily the deck's edge. Here, starting the layout at the double joist that acts as the header for the stair stringers makes much more sense than starting layout from the edge of the deck.

START THE LAYOUT FROM A LOGICAL POINT

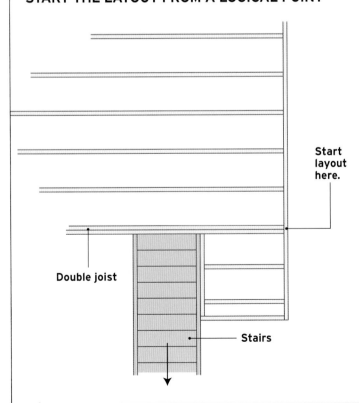

Start layout here.

Double joist

Stairs

5 Install the rim joist to the end of the ledger using 3-in. through screws.

6 Adjust the rim joist square to the house by using the 3-4-5 method or the Pythagorean theorem.

Pulling secondary layouts

Secondary layouts are all the other layouts on beams or rim joists that reference the first layout. Use the rim joist that you squared to the ledger (that is, the house) as the reference for the secondary layouts. For the joist layout parallel to the rim joist, mark the adjacent joist and pull layout from that, rather than pulling directly from the rim joist ❶. Extend the tape across the top of the beam, lock it so it won't recoil, and register it on the first joist position. Then mark the layout on the beam, moving the ladder as necessary ❷. Locking the tape frees up both hands for marking and avoids the excess hassle of having to work the tape every time you move the ladder. You could butt the tape to the rim joist instead of marking the adjacent joist, but then you'd have to move the ladder all the way down to the other end and work back to the rim. This may seem like a small difference, but many small efficiencies add up to a lot of saved work and time.

1 Register the tape on the joist layout adjacent to the rim joist and extend it the length of the beam.

2 Mark the joist layout on the top of the beam. Remember to indicate which side of the mark the joist will land on.

PULLING LAYOUT (CONTINUED)

To extend the rim-joist reference, use a string line to transfer the layout to additional beams. Tack a 2× block to the rim joist at the house ❸. Tack another 2× block to the rim joist over the first beam and then extend a string line that's aligned with the blocks to transfer the layout ❹. On this deck, the extended joists were sistered on the side with the blocks, meaning that the new joist layout was offset by 1½ in. If we were going to sister the joist to the inside, we would have put the blocks to the inside. To continue the layout across the beams, align the tape to the string and mark the layout, again noting to which side of the mark the joist will land ❺.

3 Place 2× blocks on the side of the rim joist. Place one block near the ledger and the other block over the beam.

⚠ WHAT CAN GO WRONG

It's easy to lose track of which side of the board you're pulling layout from. Once you've marked a joist, clearly indicate to which side the joist will land before marking anymore joist locations.

4 Align the string when transferring the layout to additional beams.

5 Use the string as a reference to pull additional parallel layouts.

Pulling layout on an angle

Sometimes you need to pull layout on an angle. You can use a construction calculator to figure the distance between the joists based on the Pythagorean theorem (see "Pythagorean Theorem" on p. 126), but it might be just as quick to pull a few measurements.

To figure the layout with a tape measure, hook the tape on the nearest joist and align the tape perpendicular to the joist with a Speed Square ❶. Move the tape and square along the joist until the tape reads 16 in. to the framing on the angle, in this case a rim beam ❷. Mark the joist location with a Speed Square ❸. Slide

1 When pulling layout on an angle, use a Speed Square to align the tape at a 45° angle to the last joist.

2 Measure 16 in. from the last joist, square to the rim joist, and mark the location.

3 Mark a vertical line on the rim joist to give yourself a reference when installing the field joists.

ANOTHER WAY TO LAY OUT ON AN ANGLE

Another way to figure on-center joist spacing on an angle is to extend the line of joists already installed. This method requires a level or straightedge. Align the level with the edge of the first joist and extend it over the rim joist or beam ❶. Repeat the process with the next joist over ❷. Then measure between the marks to get the on-center distance between the joist on the angle ❸.

PULLING LAYOUT (CONTINUED)

the tape and square along the joist until the tape reads 32 in. and mark another joist location ❹. Measure between the joist locations along the angle to find the on-center joist spacing ❺. Now you can use this spacing to pull layout along the angle.

If you have a long run on the angle, it's a good idea to establish joist locations at either end and pull layout to the center. If the layouts don't line up, take half the discrepancy divided by the number of spaces and this is the distance the on-center number needs to be adjusted by. For example, say there is a 2-in. gap between the layouts pulled from either end. For ease of math, say there are 8 joist spaces on either side. With simple math you know the initial on-center joist space is ⅛ in. too short. Add ⅛ in. to that number, then pull layout again and you should be dead on.

ⓘ TRADE SECRET

The bed angle of most circular saws limits a bevel cut to 45° (or sometimes 51°). To cut a bevel at a greater angle, clamp a section of beam flush to the end of the joist. To calculate the saw angle, simply subtract the desired angle from 90°. Here, I am cutting a 58° angle so I set the saw at 32°.

4 Slide the tape down and measure 32 in. from the last joist, square to the rim joist, and mark that location.

5 Measure the distance between the marks on the rim joist to discover the on-center joist distance along the rim joist.

PYTHAGOREAN THEOREM

A handy trick to have in your tool bag is the Pythagorean theorem, which states that for any right-angle triangle $a^2 + b^2 = c^2$.
For example, if a = 6 and b = 8, then c = 10.
$6^2 + 8^2 = 10^2$
$36 + 64 = 100$

$$a^2 + b^2 = c^2$$

ROLLING JOISTS

1 Sight down the joist to determine the overall quality and crown orientation. Discard any boards that are severely warped.

2 Stage the joists with one end on the beam and the crowns all facing the same direction.

3 Walk each joist up the ladder so you are in a comfortable position to hold the board when you install it.

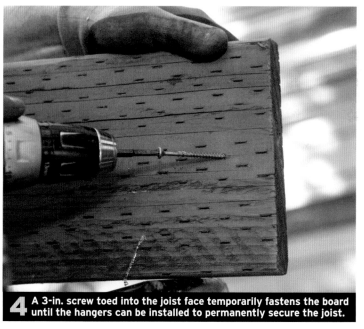

4 A 3-in. screw toed into the joist face temporarily fastens the board until the hangers can be installed to permanently secure the joist.

Installing joists, also called rolling joists, provides the support for the decking and is a satisfying process because it's the stage when the shape of the deck really starts to become apparent. There are a variety of techniques you can use when installing joists, especially when it comes to how the joist hangers are installed. There is no one right way. Here, and in the sections covering installing rim joists (see p. 138), you'll see several techniques applied to different situations. That said, all proper joist installations should involve careful lumber selection, accurate installation, and secure connections.

Before moving any joist from the delivery location down to the work zone, examine the lumber and discard any boards that are severely crowned or kinked **1**. Bowed, twisted, and slightly crowned lumber can all be dealt with at installation as long as the flaws are not extreme. While culling the lumber, make a note of the crown direction on the side of the board with a crow's foot. Carry and spread all of the material for each section and align all the crowns in the same direction **2**. Position the ladder where you can easily reach the ledger that the joists

ROLLING JOISTS (CONTINUED)

5 Align the edge of the joist to the layout mark and drive the screw to secure the joist to the ledger.

6 Move to a comfortable position for each joist installation. It is far less effort to move the ladder than it is to work from an awkward position.

7 Install the joist hangers tight to the joist with galvanized nails per the manufacturer's specifications.

WHAT CAN GO WRONG

Dimensional lumber can vary in height. If you align the joists to the bottom of the ledger, the tops—where the decking rests—may vary, leading to an uneven deck surface.

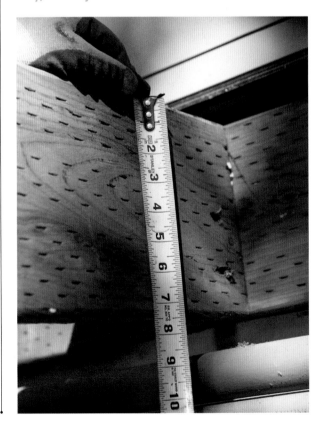

will attach to ❸ (p. 127). While holding the joist in a comfortable position, start a 3-in. screw in the face of the board near the end you want to attach ❹ (p. 127). Align the top of the joist to the ledger top while holding the joist to the layout mark and drive the screw home ❺. For now, each joist needs only two screws to hold it in place temporarily. Attach all the joists to the ledger while resting the other end on the beam ❻. If there is a chance that someone will stand on the deck joists before the decking is installed, take the time now to install the joist hangers ❼.

INSTALLING JOIST HANGERS

If the joists are in place, installing the hangers starts by setting one side of the hanger flush to the side of the joist with the bottom corner snug to the bottom edge of the joist ❶.

Tap the holding tab into the ledger to temporarily hold the hanger in place ❷.

Hold the fastener with your fingernails facing away from the hammer's head. If you miss with the hammer you are far less likely to injure yourself, although it will probably still hurt ❸.

Adjust the opposite side of the hanger until the joist is seated flush to the hanger bottom ❹.

Secure all the joist hangers to the ledger, then go back and secure the joists to the hangers. Since the nails for the latter are a different size this will save time ❺.

Drive the longer fasteners at an angle to extend from the joist-side of the flange all the way into the ledger ❻.

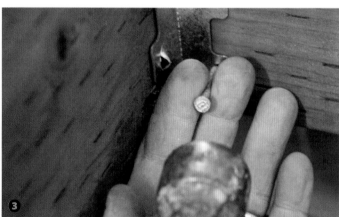

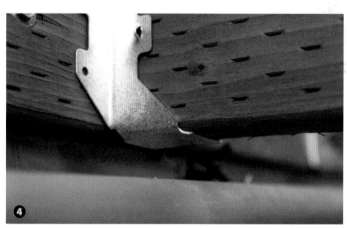

STRAIGHTENING BEAMS

The beam needs to be straightened before the joists can be secured to it. To straighten the beam, first plumb the posts that support it at either end ❶. Secure the joists closest to the ends with a screw angled through the joist face into the top of the beam ❷. Attach a 2× block to the beam's side at both ends and stretch a string line between them so the string is taut and flush to the block faces ❸. Use the distance of the beam to the line as a guide for straightening the beam ❹. When the beam is straight and in position, secure the joists to the beam with 3-in. screws or galvanized nails ❺. If the beam has a serious bow to it, you may have to hold it straight until you can fasten all the joists.

1 Check the posts at either end of the beam for plumb. If necessary, adjust the bracing to return the posts to plumb.

2 Fasten the end joist to the top of the beam to hold each end while straightening the beam.

3 Stretch a string between 2× blocks that are attached under each secured joist. Take care that the string is flush to the block faces.

4 Adjust the beam until it is a consistent distance from the string along the entire length.

5 Secure the beam in position by attaching the joists to the beam's top.

TRADE SECRET

Use a block instead of a measuring tape to gauge the distance from the string to the beam. With a block, it is easier to see how much space to make up to get the beam straight.

STRAIGHTENING BEAMS (CONTINUED)

Working around joists

Once the joists are installed, it's time to move the base of operations up to the level of the deck. Even if the deck you are working on is only a few feet above grade, it's well worth the time spent to install some planks or plywood to make moving around on the joists safe and easy. If you have some reject joists, these make great planks. To be safe, secure the plank to a joist at both ends. Also, a sheet of plywood makes a great staging area for tools and materials. For safety, fasten the plywood edge to a joist and run any ladders up at least 3 ft. beyond the deck's elevation.

WHAT CAN GO WRONG

Don't walk on unblocked joists. Even if the joists are secured, the lateral force of walking on the tops could be enough to wrench them loose. Wait until the planks are on and the blocking is installed before putting any force on the top of the joists.

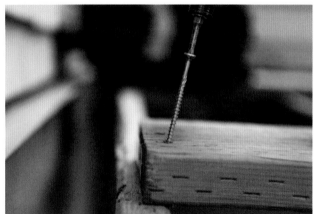

Use rejected joists as temporary deck planks to make navigating over the top of joists easier and safer.

Fasten temporary deck planking to the joists with screws. Make sure that both ends of the plank are fully supported by a joist.

Organize tools and materials on the level you will need them. As with planking, fasten the plywood to the joist with screws and check to make sure it is fully supported and will support the weight of people and tools.

1 Measure the distance between joists and adjust any joists that are more than 1/4 in. off layout.

2 Mark a board at 14 1/2-in. intervals. If necessary, mark a square line across the board face to align the sawblade as you cut.

3 Cut to the inside of the line. This will leave you with blocking that is 14 7/16 in. long, or thereabouts.

4 Cut all the blocking using the same method and at the same time to increase efficiency.

Adding blocking

Blocking, sometimes called crush blocking, is installed to keep the joists upright and to prevent them from rolling to the side under load. Blocking is another good use of joists that were rejected previously. In its simplest terms, installing blocking is just filling the gap between two joists. That said, there are as many blocks to install as there are joists and if done correctly the job is efficient and

not too time consuming. On the other hand, if approached haphazardly, installing the blocks can take a frustratingly long time. Over the years we have developed a system that gets the job done correctly and quickly.

To begin, double-check to make sure the space between the joists is a consistent 14 1/2 in. **1**. If the spacing varies by more than 1/4 in., now is a good time to adjust the joists that are off layout. Cutting the block-

ing at exactly 14 1/2 in. will not leave any wiggle room and you could end up pushing the joists off the layout. To prevent this, cut the blocking at 14 7/16 in. There's an easy way to do this. Measure and mark an entire board at 14 1/2-in. intervals **2**. Using a circular saw, cut to the short side of the line, taking the line as you cut **3**. This will result in blocks that are about 1/16 in. shy. Cut all the blocks at one time **4**. Treat the ends of the blocks

STRAIGHTENING BEAMS (CONTINUED)

5 Dip each end of the cut blocks in wood preservative to protect them from rot and insect damage.

6 Use a square to mark the joist face where it intersects the beam face.

7 Measure over 1½ in. to mark the location of the line to which the blocks will be aligned.

8 Mark the joist at the other end in the same manner and snap a chalkline along the joist tops.

WHAT CAN GO WRONG

Check the blade thickness. If you are using a chopsaw, be aware that most chopsaw blades are thicker than a hand-held circular saw and your blocks may end up too short.

with wood preservative and set them aside to let the preservative dry before installing **5**.

To lay out for the block installation, square up from the beam's edge inside the last joist **6**. This line represents one side of the blocking; it can be used to reference the blocking installation by setting all the blocking to the inside of the line. However, we prefer to measure over 1½ in. and mark a crow's foot to reference the chalkline **7**. This does two things. First, it gives you two points of reference. You can sight down the face of the block and beam as well as align the edge to the line. It also allows an in-line installation over the beam or a staggered installation. Repeat the same layout process on the other end of the blocking run and

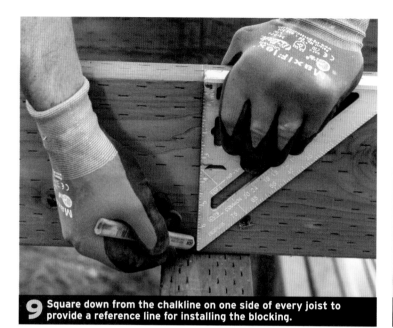

9 Square down from the chalkline on one side of every joist to provide a reference line for installing the blocking.

10 Through-screw the blocking where possible. Use at least two screws per end to secure the blocking.

11 Angle the screws to secure the blocking where necessary. Sight down from above to effectively align the screw.

12 Check the blocks to make sure the tops do not extend above the joists, which would create a hump in the decking.

snap a line along the joist tops **8**. On one side of the joist, mark a plumb line down from the chalk mark to help align the block during installation **9**.

To install, align the block to the marks and through-screw (or nail) one end **10**. The plan for this deck called for more joists to be sistered on at the beam. For this situation, the blocking needs to be installed in line to allow the end of the sistered joist to rest on the beam top. This means that at one end of the blocking, the screws have to be angled in **11**. This is just as strong as running them straight in but takes a little more time. Take care to make sure that the blocking sits flush with the joist top **12**. If necessary, trim any blocking that sits proud; otherwise, it will create a bump in the decking.

STRAIGHTENING BEAMS (CONTINUED)

STAGGER BLOCKING IF YOU CAN

Staggering blocks is easier that installing them in line as it allows both ends to be fastened without angling the screw.

TRADE SECRET

Secure the chalkline with an awl point instead of a nail. I had the great fortune of working alongside *Fine Homebuilding* icon Larry Haun, and he showed me this trick of using an awl to hold a chalkline. It's much faster than digging out a nail and pounding it in place, and cheaper than hiring a helper.

SISTERING JOISTS

To extend a run beyond common joist length, the joists need to be sistered to each other. It's important to remember that sistering joists is not a load-bearing arrangement but rather is used for alignment. Sistering is done so that all the joists are adequately supported by the beam. Also the framing has to be designed so that one run of joists extends beyond the beam by 2 ft. We like to run the first set of joists over the beam. That way we can install the blocking before sistering the joists.

Before fastening a joist, hold it in place and check to make sure the tops can be aligned ❶. If the joist to be added is too tall, trim the bottom until it sits flush to the first joist. Fasten the joist with 3-in. screws or galvanized nails driven at a slight angle to prevent the tips from protruding on the other side ❷. Use a schedule five pattern to permanently secure the joist ❸.

FASTENING PATTERNS

A common fastening pattern for face-nailing or face-screwing joists is a schedule five, or domino, pattern.

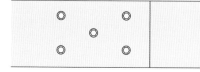

Fasteners in the schedule five pattern

1 Position the joist adjacent to the installed joist with the end butted to the blocking.

2 Ensure the tops are flush and fasten the joists together by slightly angling a 3-in. or 3½-in. fastener.

3 Secure the sistered joist with a schedule five, or domino, fastening pattern.

INSTALLING RIM JOISTS

There are a few different ways to install rim joists depending on the situation. Here, we will discuss two ways to install rim joists that run perpendicular to the field joists and one way to install a rim joist that runs parallel.

Method 1: Through screwing

When a beam supports the joists from below, securing the rim joist to the field joists with through screws will save time over using hangers. Also, in this situation hangers are redundant because the rim joist carries little weight. The main function of the rim joist here is to keep the joists aligned.

Pull and mark the joist layout on the inside face of the rim joist ❶ and then extend the layout lines down the rim joist's face and over the top ❷. Be sure to mark which side of the line the field joist falls to and then start a 3-in. screw to fasten the rim joist to the field joist ❸. If you're working alone, start this screw in the middle so you can balance the rim joist while holding it for the installation. Align the top of the field joist with one hand and drive the screw to secure the rim joist ❹. Align the field joist to the layout mark you made on the inside face and then permanently secure the rim joist with two more fasteners ❺. Finally, align and secure the rim joist to the rest of the field joists with through screws in the same manner.

1 Measure and mark the joist layout on the rim joist, remembering to indicate which side of the mark the joist will fall.

2 Use a square to extend the layout marks across the face and top of the joist.

3 Start the first screw near the top of a middle joist based on the layout marks you made on the face.

4 Align the rim top to the joist and fasten it to the joist with a screw.

5 Fasten the rim joist permanently to the joist with two more through screws.

 **WHAT CAN GO WRONG**

If the joists are attached to the beam, you may be fighting to get everything perfectly lined up. To correct this, loosen the top screw to realign the joist plumb.

INSTALLING RIM JOISTS (CONTINUED)

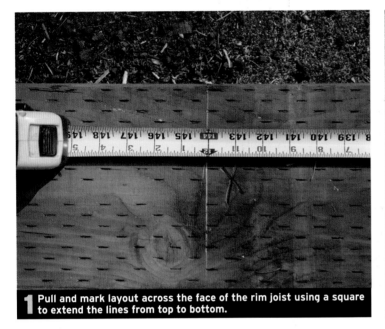

1 Pull and mark layout across the face of the rim joist using a square to extend the lines from top to bottom.

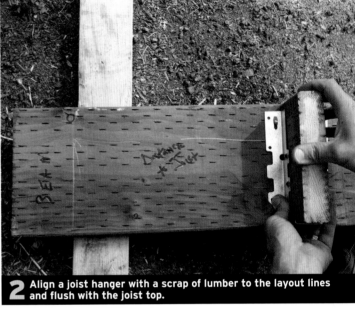

2 Align a joist hanger with a scrap of lumber to the layout lines and flush with the joist top.

3 Depress the hanger tab to hold the joist in the right position.

4 Drive 1¼-in. Teco nails through the hanger holes to secure it to the rim joist.

Method 2: Installing hangers

If it's not convenient to stand on the outside of the rim joist to through-screw the fasteners, installing hangers to the rim joist before fastening it in position is a good option. Two key points with this method are to make sure that layout is as accurate as possible and to check that the rim joists don't vary in height by more than 1/16 in.

To install the field joists this way, begin by pulling layout across the inside rim joist face and mark the side of the layout that the field joist falls to **1**. Use an end cut that matches the joist's dimension to align the joist hanger on the layout **2**. When the top of the end cut is flush with the top of the rim joist, drive the hanger's tab to hold it in place and then drive 1¼-in. nails into the hanger holes to

secure the hanger **3**. Install all the hangers per the layout and then install the rim joist, fitting the field joists into the hanger **4**.

1 Find the length of the end rim joist by hooking the tape and measuring from outside to outside.

2 Attach a block to the bottom of the adjacent rim joist to act as a third hand.

3 Position the rim joist on the block while attaching the other end.

4 Through-screw the rim joist with 3½-in. screws to permanently secure it and then remove the block.

Method 3: Parallel rim joist

When a rim joist runs parallel to the field joists, the installation can be quick and uncomplicated. Once the adjacent rim joists are installed and fully secured, measure between them for the rim-joist length **1**. If you are approaching the installation from above or working alone, secure a block to the underside of the adjacent joist to act as a third-hand helper **2**. Use the block to support one side of the rim joist while you install the other side **3**. Last, secure the end supported by the block with 3-in. through screws **4**.

INSTALLING DECKING

THE OLD SAYING THAT THE PROOF is in the pudding aptly applies to installing decking on the frame. If, while framing the deck, you've taken care to square the structure, align the joist tops, and install fasteners flush, that attention to detail will ease the process of installing the decking with professional-grade results. The basic installation steps are similar regardless of what materials and fasteners you use. That said, some materials and fasteners will take double or triple the time to install compared to the more typical options.

In this chapter, you'll learn the basic preparations you need to make to start the install off right as well as learn how to gap boards properly, deal with an out-of-square frame, and add a picture-frame border for a more professional look. We'll also review installation techniques for different styles of fasteners and explain how to detail your deck with fascia and decking patterns to enhance its visual appeal.

GENERAL PREPARATION

Practical Considerations, p. 144

INSTALLING DECKING

ADDING FASCIA AND OTHER DECORATIVE ELEMENTS

PRACTICAL CONSIDERATIONS

As with all phases of deck building, staging your building materials and fasteners ahead of time will help the process go smoothly. Also, make sure to give the framing a once-over to check for joists that aren't aligned, fasteners that protrude, or other details that need to be buttoned up. It is much easier to correct flaws in the framing before the decking installation begins.

Installing decking is a repetitive job and takes a surprisingly long time, so if you have some people to help who are good with detail and have some basic DIY skills, now's a good time to call them in. You'll also appreciate their help when moving and staging materials. Most decking comes in lengths up to 16 ft., and it can be a challenge for one person to navigate the job site while carrying these boards. In addition, depending on the material, it may be impossible for one person to do the job—some types of synthetic decking are so floppy that both ends touch the ground even when hoisted up on your shoulder.

The type of decking will also determine the tools you'll need. Deck fasteners often have specific bits or driver attachments that need to be purchased along with the materials, and you will want to identify these and purchase them well in advance.

If the decking material is rough, like a natural softwood, crosscutting the lengths with a handheld circular saw will often be sufficient. To improve the cut accuracy with a circular saw, you can use it in combination with a Speed Square or crosscut jig.

Hardwood decking and some types of synthetic materials, especially those that mimic hardwoods, have tighter tolerances for installations. In these situations you'll want to consider setting up a chopsaw station to make accurate cuts quickly.

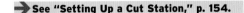

➡ See "Setting Up a Cut Station," p. 154.

Installing decking requires some logistical considerations, such as where to store it and how best to move it around the site.

Finally, you'll need to consider material flow when setting up the staging and cutting areas. Try to set up your process so the material will move lengthwise from station to station. It will slow you down considerably to have to turn the long boards when carrying them from the staging pile to the cutting station and then to the deck for installation.

Before you begin

Before any decking goes down, you'll need to decide on any special features you may want to include and install the proper framing to support the design. Some common enhancements are adding a picture-frame border, varying the width of the deck boards, adding fascia boards to the outside framing, and installing a herringbone pattern where perpendicular runs of deck boards intersect.

Another task to complete before installing decking is layout. With layout, the goal is to determine exactly how many deck boards will fill a given run and to adjust the gap between boards to avoid having to install a partial piece of decking.

A herringbone pattern is an attractive way to intersect two sections of decking that have perpendicular deck boards. Here, the picture frame on the right becomes part of the deck pattern on the left.

WHAT YOU'LL NEED

Installing decking requires only a few tools. You'll need a saw to cut the boards to length and another to scribe the boards around posts. Beyond that, you really need only a driver for fasteners and an assortment of hand tools.

- Circular saw or chopsaw
- Jigsaw
- Drill driver
- Bits
- Basic hand tools

PRACTICAL CONSIDERATIONS (CONTINUED)

A picture-frame border runs perpendicular to the field decking. On this deck, the borders visually tie together the deck and the wraparound steps.

Framing for a picture-frame border

One of the features that can significantly upgrade a deck's appearance is a picture-frame border. A picture frame is easy to construct and consists of decking boards installed around the perimeter of the deck and perpendicular to the field boards at the sides. At the corners, the deck boards are mitered or lapped, depending on personal preference.

➡ See "Installing a Picture-Frame Border," p. 152.

To add framing for a picture-frame border, begin by cutting a series of spacers from 1/2-in. pressure-treated plywood ❶ (the spacers create a drainage gap). Cut each spacer 3 in. wide and just a little shorter than the width of the framing lumber. For example, if the joist is a 2×8, cut the spacer to 7 3/8 in. At one end of the spacer, cut the corners at 45° to form a point. When installed, this point will shed water off the top of the spacer and help prevent rot. Cut enough spacers to allow for one spacer every 4 ft. along the length of the run. Attach the spacers along the inside of a doubled rim joist with a single screw through the spacer's middle ❷. Over the spacers, add a joist to the inside of the existing joists; this joist will help support the ends of the field decking ❸. Secure this joist along the face with two 3-in. screws through each spacer ❹. Then secure the joist through the end with three screws through the adjacent framing ❺.

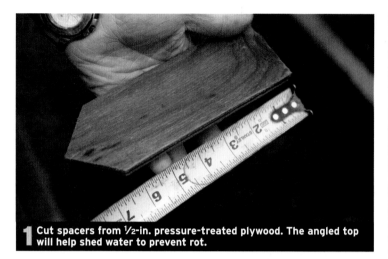

1 Cut spacers from ½-in. pressure-treated plywood. The angled top will help shed water to prevent rot.

2 Fasten the spacers to the doubled rim joist every 3 ft. to 4 ft. Align the top flush with, but not above, the top of the joists.

3 Place a third joist to the inside. This joist will help support the ends of the field decking.

4 Secure the joist with 3½-in. screws at the spacer locations.

5 Secure the joist at the end with 3-in. screws through the adjacent joist. Be sure to align the joist tops to avoid bumps in the decking.

TRADE SECRET
To prevent problems when installing the decking, take care to make sure that the spacers don't extend above the top of the joists.

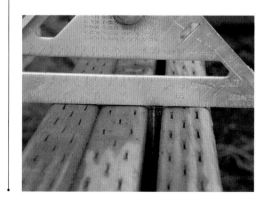

ESTABLISHING A LAYOUT

When installing decking, there are three basic options of where to begin: at the house, at the perimeter of the deck, or in the middle at a plank that spans from one part of the deck to another. Starting at the house has the advantage that it is easier to install the board adjacent to the building before it is trapped by the other deck boards. If you've got a long run and don't need to tie into other portions of the deck, this is the most common starting point (it's not our preference, though).

The advantage of starting at the perimeter (as shown in the photo sequence on the facing page) is that you can precisely space the picture frame and field boards for a refined look. Any adjustment can then happen at the house, where it will be less noticeable. Starting in the middle and working both toward the perimeter and the house can be a good strategy when one board connects two layouts (see "Starting Layout in the Middle" at right).

STARTING LAYOUT IN THE MIDDLE

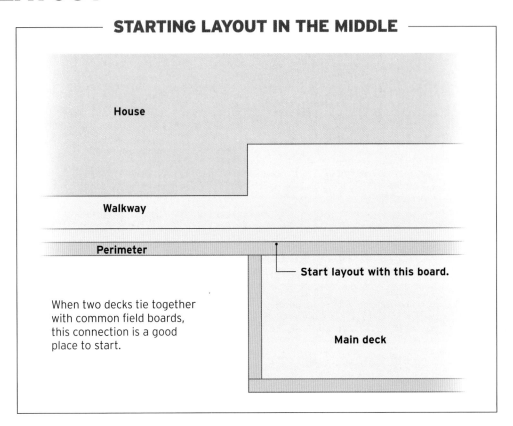

When two decks tie together with common field boards, this connection is a good place to start.

MIND THE GAP

The standard gap for decking boards is plus or minus ¼ in., depending on conditions. For example, if you are installing a well-seasoned decking material in a stable environment that does not change in moisture content between the seasons, you can get away with less of a gap. In a wet environment, on the other hand, you'll likely require a greater gap. Ask the manufacturer or supplier for guidelines in your area.

1 Mark the perimeter board's final position. Use the combination of the overhang and fascia thickness to locate the perimeter board.

2 Measure the overall distance for the decking layout. Each section of decking will require a slightly different set of calculations.

3 Reference your measurements from the farthest point from the perimeter. In this case, the farthest point was under the door trim.

4 Divide the overall distance by the width of a deck board plus the gap. Here, the gap was $3/16$ in. so we divided by $5^3/8$ in.

Starting at the perimeter

By adjusting the gap between the boards, you can prevent the need to split a plank of decking at the end of a run. To lay out a run, place the last plank in position with the correct overhang to account for any fascia **1**. Here, we used a $3/4$-in. fascia with a $1^1/4$-in. overhang for a total of a 2-in. overhang from the framing. While we're at it, we mark the

board's edge to use as a reference. From the edge of this board, measure back to the building to determine the overall run **2**. Make sure to measure from exactly where you want the first plank to start. Here, we opted to start the measurement from the flashing under the trim **3**. However, different situations call for different strategies (see "What Can Go Wrong," on p. 151).

Once you know the overall run, simply divide that distance by the measurement of one plank and one space **4**. For this deck we used $3/16$-in. plastic spacers that wouldn't compress. Many people like to use a construction pencil to gap the boards, but pencils are made of softwood and will compress as the deck progresses, changing the gap. An alternative is to cut hardwood

ESTABLISHING A LAYOUT (CONTINUED)

5 Cut custom hardwood spacers to help reduce error in measuring and to keep the layout on track.

TRADE SECRET

It's worth investing in some plywood to lay over exposed joists while you're installing decking. You will more than make back the cost of the plywood in time saved.

6 Check the progress against the layout to ensure that the calculations are accurate.

spacers from scrap **5**. A trick to get a more accurate estimate is to measure across several planks and spaces **6**. This limits the errors caused by variations of an individual board. For a short run of decking you may not be able to have an even number of planks. In that case, use a partial plank against the house. With longer runs, only a small difference in the gap will give you enough flexibility to have an even number of boards. It's not necessary to mark the layout of every board in a run. Instead, mark intervals of 5 or 10 boards, so you can check the progress and make corrections if you get off track.

WHAT CAN GO WRONG

In a perfect world, there would be no undulating or out-of-square walls. Fortunately, there are some almost-foolproof fixes that will handle most of the less-than-ideal situations. For undulating walls, use a partial plank adjacent to the wall and scribe it to fit (see the top drawing below).

For an out-of-square deck, make up the difference by adjusting the gap between the boards in small increments (see the bottom drawing below). For severely out-of-square decks, you may have to use a combination of the two strategies.

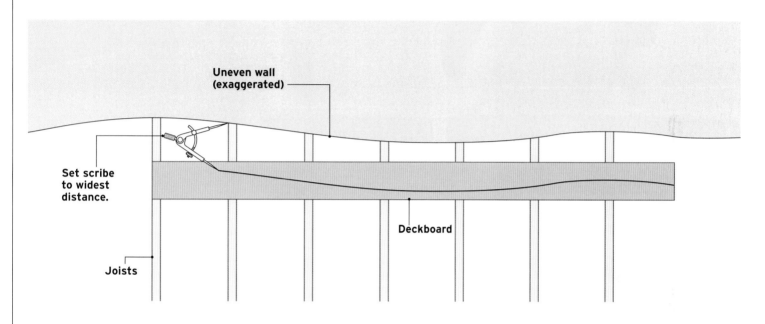

Uneven wall
(exaggerated)

Set scribe
to widest
distance.

Deckboard

Joists

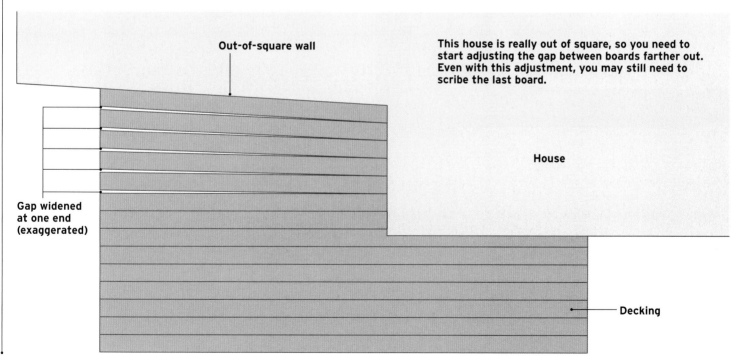

Out-of-square wall

This house is really out of square, so you need to start adjusting the gap between boards farther out. Even with this adjustment, you may still need to scribe the last board.

House

Gap widened
at one end
(exaggerated)

Decking

INSTALLING A PICTURE-FRAME BORDER

1 Calculate the overhang from the framing by adding the desired overhang to the fascia thickness.

2 Snap a chalkline on the layout for the inside edge of the perimeter board.

3 Add the deck width plus two times the overhang to calculate the end board of the picture frame.

4 Mark the fastener locations using a Speed Square and an awl. Typically, the perimeter boards will require top-screw fasteners.

5 Countersink the fastener heads below the decking surface to avoid splinters and a general messiness.

If you choose to surround your deck with a picture-frame border, it can be installed before or after the field decking. One technique is to install the field decking first, letting the ends run long then cut them all at once to accommodate the border. The advantage of this method is that it saves time over cutting and fitting each board to length. The disadvantage is the increased risk of tearout from the circular saw at the board ends. Also, if you've chosen to round the corners of the butt cut, you'll spend extra time on your knees making those cuts. Unless pressed for time, we like

to install the border first because we find we get better results when we cut the ends and round the edges individually.

Usually every section of the deck gets a border, but the steps are the same for large and small sections alike. The first step is to establish the overhang, which depends on the thickness of the fascia material you choose. To establish the overhang from the framing, add the desired overhang, typically ³⁄₄ in. to 1¹⁄₄ in., to the fascia's thickness. For the deck shown here, a 1¹⁄₄-in. overhang with a ³⁄₄-in. fascia equaled a 2-in. overhang

from the framing **1**. Mark the edge of the decking board on both ends and then snap a chalkline across the framing to mark the board's edge **2**. Measure and cut the end board to length, remembering to add enough for the overhang, in this case 4 in. (2 in. for each side) **3**.

Depending on the fastener system, part or the entire border will require top screwing. Three simple techniques will help keep the appearance of the top screws clean. First, use a Speed Square to align the holes across the board **4**. While it is easy enough

6 Predrill and drive fasteners to secure the perimeter. For hardwoods, use a small-headed fastener.

7 Locate the perimeter's side boards. If the side of the deck is longer than a few feet, locate and snap a chalkline.

8 Align the corner with a spacer and square. Any deviations in the pattern will be more noticeable at the corners.

9 Secure the perimeter board at the corner first. Predrill and drive fasteners through the face.

10 Check for square before fastening the rest of the perimeter board.

to hit the framing below by just eyeballing the fastener location, the uniformity of the fasteners' locations adds a sense of order to the deck that is subliminal yet effective. To avoid splinters and messy tearout, countersink the screw heads **5**. Later you can decide to plug the holes and sand them flush or leave them as they are. Also to avoid splitting hardwoods, it's a good idea to predrill all fastener holes. Finally, if you're installing hardwood, use a small-headed fastener and matching countersink **6**. For softwoods you'll have to use a standard

deck fastener to prevent the head from pulling through. While securing the board, reference the chalkline you snapped earlier.

Once the end board is installed, measure and cut the sides of the picture frame **7**. The length of the side board will match the measurement you took for layout. Align the sides with a spacer and Speed Square **8**. Then secure the end with the same top-screw method **9**. Before fastening the loose end, square the picture frame using the 3-4-5 method (see p. 72) **10**.

TRADE SECRET

Instead of measuring the overhang with a tape, cut a block that matches the overhang from the framing. The gauge block is much quicker to use than pulling out the tape and provides both a visual and tactile way to ensure the decking is positioned correctly.

SETTING UP A CUT STATION

It's well worth taking a few minutes to set up a chopsaw cut station. A simple cut station like the one described here has a positive stop that enables you to repeat cuts without measuring each board. This is crucial for hardwood decks with small tolerances, where small variations in board length can easily be noticed. Even for softwood decks, a cut station will allow for quick, accurate cuts.

To set up a cutting station, first secure a chopsaw to a stable surface that provides support to the long deck planks ❶. Two sawhorses set apart will do, but often a section of framing will work perfectly because it is very easy to break down and move this station. To support the deck planks while cutting, we typically use a reject board blocked up to the height of the chopsaw deck ❷. However, if the deck planking is a full 1½ in. thick, we will opt for a thinner piece of stock as a support. Secure the other end of the support board to the chopsaw deck by clamping or screwing it to the fence ❸. Make sure to overlap the board's end enough to make a fresh cut with the chopsaw once the board is secured in place ❹. This cut is now the reference point to set your stops from.

To set the stop, hook the tape on the fresh cut and measure back the length of the decking you want to install ❺. Mark this spot and use that mark as a reference to secure a stop in the proper location ❻. To make a cut, simply set the uncut plank onto your support board and align the end to the stop. It's a good idea to make a test cut to check that the station is set up correctly ❼.

Chose an area for the cut station **that can accommodate long boards and that won't be in the way.**

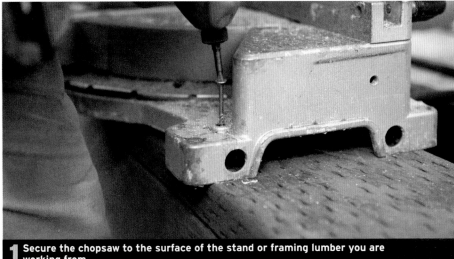

1 Secure the chopsaw to the surface of the stand or framing lumber you are working from.

2 Use a ¾-in. plank as the supporting surface. On the infeed side, raise the plank with blocks the same thickness as the chopsaw base.

3 Secure the other side to the chopsaw base and fence with clamps or screws. Double-check to make sure the plank is aligned.

4 Cut off the excess support plank. If the plank doesn't extend across the cut zone, readjust the plank until it does and cut off the excess.

5 Measure back from the fresh cut of the support plank to the desired length of the board to be cut.

6 Secure a stop to the mark to make repeated cuts at one length.

7 Cut the desired number of boards to length.

INSTALLING DECK PLANKS

The basic steps of installing deck planks are not difficult. Cutting planks to length, spacing them correctly, and securing them are all operations that anyone with limited DIY experience can easily accomplish. The difficulty comes in the repetition. Not only will you repeat these operations ad nauseam, but you will also need to keep your focus so you repeat them correctly from beginning to end.

When measuring for field boards remember to account for the spacing on both ends of the board. To secure the boards on this deck, we opted for a fastening system developed by Kreg, which is famous for its pocket-screw systems. We have used many different types of hidden fastener systems and found this system to be among the best for both ease of use and fastening ability.

Whether you are using this system or another type, the general steps are the same. First, position the board and align the spacers ❶. Check the gaps at both ends to make sure that the board length is correct. If there is a bow to the board, orient the board so the bow pushes the ends away from the adjacent plank. This way you will always be pushing the board into place instead of trying to pull it. Align and fasten one end of the board to begin the installation ❷. Once the end is secure, slide the spacer down to the next joist, push the deck board tight to the spacer, and fasten it in place ❸. Periodically check both what has been installed and what is left to be installed to ensure that the calculated layout is accurate ❹.

1 Use spacers to align the board. If the board has a bow, orient the arch toward the adjacent board already installed.

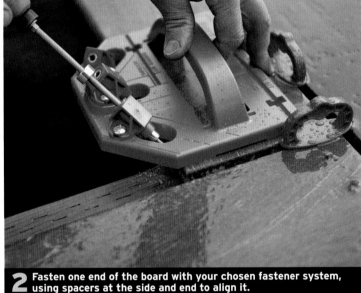

2 Fasten one end of the board with your chosen fastener system, using spacers at the side and end to align it.

3 Continue fastening the board at each joist location. The more consistent you are with your process, the neater it will be.

4 Check your progress every couple of boards to make sure that you are on layout and make any necessary adjustments.

5 Place spacers at each joist location. If the board is bowed, keep the spacers in place while securing the adjacent joist.

6 Use bar clamps to pull a board with a more drastic bow into alignment.

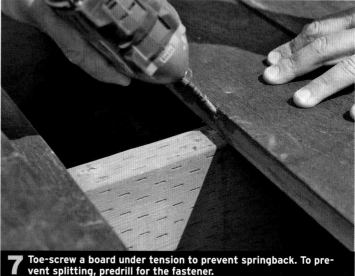

7 Toe-screw a board under tension to prevent springback. To prevent splitting, predrill for the fastener.

For wide decks with runs of longer planks, use multiple spacers across several fastening points **5**. This will help the work go faster and even out variations of individual boards. If a plank has a bow to it and needs to be pushed or pulled into place, a bar clamp can apply a significant amount of persuasion **6**. If you don't have a clamp long enough to hook the edge of the deck, try reversing the clamp so it's pushing instead of pulling. To hold a board in place under tension, predrill and toe-screw the plank from the side **7**.

Measure the board length **and make the adjustment to account for the gaps at either end. Also if you haven't done so already, take measurements for the first and last board to ensure they are equal.**

INSTALLING DECK PLANKS (CONTINUED)

TRADE SECRET

The flat end of a cat's paw is a great tool to use to gently pry two boards apart if the gap needs to be widened. To narrow the gap, pound the cat's paw into the joist top adjacent to the plank and pry the board until the gap narrows the desired amount. Sometimes you may need to overcompensate to allow for some springback once the board is secured.

INSTALLING HIDDEN FASTENERS

Most hidden fasteners secure the deck boards by mounting to a groove in the side ❶. While there are many variations on the theme, the basic sequence is the same. Each fastener secures the edges of two adjacent boards. Some manufacturers of composite and synthetic decking require proprietary fasteners, while many hardwood suppliers mill a groove in the side that will accommodate a variety of after-market fasteners. If you are not confused yet, get ready.

The number of generic and brand-name fasteners available, combined with how they interface with the available brands of decking, can be dizzying. To wade through the madness start by identifying the deck-ing you want and then ask the manufacturer or supplier which fastening systems will work. That will significantly cut down the options you'll need to consider. Thankfully, the installation steps for side-mounted hidden fasteners are similar.

To install a basic fastener, secure the fastener in the open groove ❷. Fit the adjacent board in place so the fasteners seat in both slots ❸. Install the fasteners in the open slot ❹. Some fastener systems require the additional step of then back-tracking and driving the fastener hidden between the boards into its final position ❺. Another variation includes a clip system that does not require any backtracking ❻.

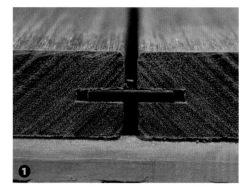

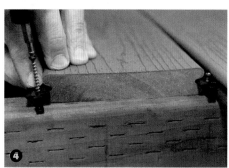

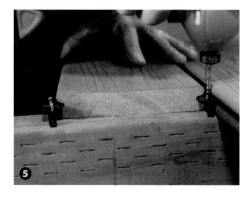

WHAT CAN GO WRONG

Mental fatigue triggered by repetition can cause you to cut corners, to skip steps in the process, or simply to make a mistake like cutting a board to the wrong length or gouging the face with a drill driver. Take enough breaks to remain focused and motivated.

ALTERNATIVES TO USING CLIPS AS HIDDEN FASTENERS

In some situations, you may need to look beyond clips for hidden-fastener options. Deckmaster makes strips that mount to the side of the joist ❶ and to the underside of the deck plank ❷. The advantage of this system is that you are not limited to the sides of the board for locating your fastener and if a fastener strips out, it's an easy fix to simply drive another fastener. This system works well with hardwood decking, which tends to exert a lot of force with seasonal wood movement.

As mentioned, Kreg makes a side-mounting fastener system, and this style is gaining popularity as other manufacturers begin to copy Kreg's success ❸.

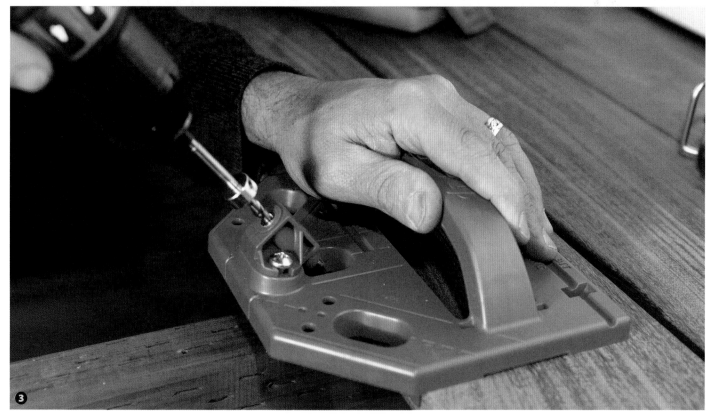

ADDING FASCIA

There are many ways to dress up a deck. Beyond the materials you choose (including the railing, which we'll discuss in the next chapter), adding fascia to cover the framing and using different patterns of decking are the two easiest ways to upgrade the look of your deck without sending the cost into the stratosphere.

Adding fascia will certainly upgrade the look of almost any deck, but it will also increase the time, effort, and cost that go into construction. As with the choices for decking, the choices for fascia are extensive but don't have to be overwhelming. The options basically fall into two camps: one is materials, and the other is design. With design, the options are nearly limitless, but we have come up with some guidelines to keep the chaos at bay.

First, we like to install a multipiece fascia. While this can increase installation time, it has several advantages. First, buying fascia wide enough to cover 8-in. or 10-in. dimensional lumber can be expensive. We try to design the fascia so we can cut it from the same lumber we used for the decking. That way, any pieces that we reject as decking can be put to use as fascia. Finally, with multipiece fascia, the dimensions can be adjusted to fit the area that needs to be covered, and because it's made from the same material as the decking it contributes to the unified look of the project.

Design a fascia detail that is attractive to you yet easy to install and adjustable to the different deck details you have on your project.

Create a unified look by using deck-board rejects resawn for the fascia material.

ADDING PATTERNS

Adding decorative decking patterns can serve two purposes. It upgrades the appearance and it can serve a functional goal. For example, adding a ¾-in. strip between the planks on stairs is a great way to achieve a comfortable run. Once that motif is introduced into the deck design, it not only becomes a design element but also provides a back door when measurements are not in your favor. On the deck shown here, the space where the two sections came together could be filled only by a partial plank. However, because of the pattern introduced in the steps, the partial board looks intentional rather than necessary. The last place on this deck that we used the decking pattern to our advantage was where the steps wrapped around the perimeter. Here, a variation of a herringbone design creates a natural transition between the perpendicular runs and is much easier to install than trying to align mitered ends.

Locate the filler strip one or two boards into the field to make it look like part of the design.

Add a filler strip on stair treads to create a design detail that can be repeated throughout the deck.

Use a herringbone pattern to weave two sections of perpendicular decking.

INSTALLING RAILINGS

DECK RAILINGS MUST BE DONE right for two reasons: for looks and for safety. An ugly railing system can make a great deck look like a dog, and if installed poorly, even a great-looking railing can be the cause of serious injury or even death. The importance of railing safety cannot be overemphasized. We literally trust them with our lives, and this expectation of safety makes the decks we build habitable.

Decks that are close to the ground or that otherwise present no risk of falling off the edge don't need a railing. For all other decks, the railing systems need to be secured to the framing and constructed in a way that conforms to the strict guidelines called for in the building codes. These codes vary between municipalities, but usually the code conforms to the IRC. In this chapter, you'll learn how to attach railing posts to deck framing, build and install a balustrade, add a railing cap, and install stair railings.

BUILDING A CODE-COMPLIANT RAILING

By the time railings are installed in a normal deck construction schedule, you've already done much of the mental preparation in terms of understanding deck structure and tuning up any skills necessary to complete the job. You will want to double-check the deck plans to make sure that any changes still allow for the railing system to be installed as planned. If there have been major changes, you'll want to reconcile the existing conditions with the deck plans before you begin the installation.

Installing traditional wood railing systems is a straightforward job, and the materials can be purchased off-the-shelf at most building centers. Composite, synthetic, and hybrid systems like cable rail have varying degrees of complexity. While there are some similarities, many of the installation details of these systems are specific to the manufacturers.

Not all decks need railing systems. Grade-level decks with wraparound stairs may not require a continuous railing.

Handrails (also called grab rails) must conform to certain profiles outlined in the code.

Guardrails and handrails are measured for height from the stair nosing.

Railings are assemblies of posts, rails, caps, and balusters

Each part of the railing assembly has a specific task. Being familiar with the different parts and how they interact will allow you not only to build a solid railing but also to add custom features that still conform to code.

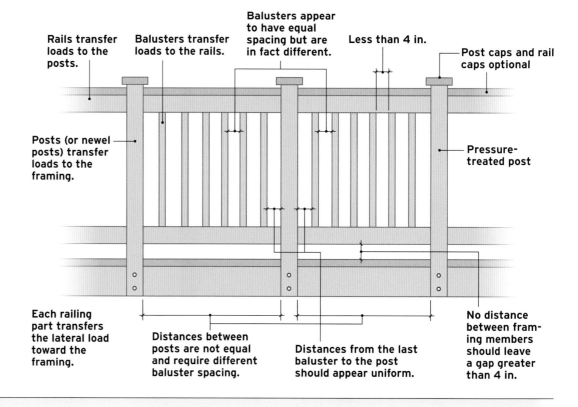

Rails transfer loads to the posts.

Balusters transfer loads to the rails.

Balusters appear to have equal spacing but are in fact different.

Less than 4 in.

Post caps and rail caps optional

Posts (or newel posts) transfer loads to the framing.

Pressure-treated post

Each railing part transfers the lateral load toward the framing.

Distances between posts are not equal and require different baluster spacing.

Distances from the last baluster to the post should appear uniform.

No distance between framing members should leave a gap greater than 4 in.

NONWOOD RAILINGS

As with decking, most railing systems are built with wood. However, the proliferation of nonwood railing systems is ever increasing the viable choices. Some manufacturers of synthetic decking offer composite railing materials that match their decking. The construction techniques for composite railing materials are often the same as for wood. Other railing systems are complete kits that have manufacturer-specific attachments to secure the components and can be combined with almost any decking material. Still others are somewhere in the middle, providing kits with parts that are designed to cleanly interface with off-the-shelf parts like newel posts or caps. We've included information about material types here as it pertains to specific railing types. For more general information on materials, see "Tools and Materials," p. 38.

Cable-rail systems **can actually enhance the view.**

Hardware allows the cables **to be adjusted for tension seasonally.**

Cable-rail systems

Cable rail is a hybrid type of system that usually combines wooden newel posts and caps with metal cable rails. With this system, long cables are passed horizontally though a series of newel posts. At each end of the cable, nuts secure the cable to the post while tensioners allow seasonal slack to be removed from the cables.

Cable systems don't obstruct the view as much as traditional wood systems. They also add an elegant touch of modernism to a deck's appearance. For a variation on the traditional look, cables can also be run vertically between metal top and bottom rails.

Cable-rail systems allow for creative applications

Second only to a site-built railing system, cable rails allow you to customize how the assembly will look. The typical cable rail system arrives in a box that contains only the cables and the hardware to attach it. The style and configuration of the post rails and caps are up to you. You could choose to construct the posts and rails from wood with a traditional look or you could choose from the many available metal-fabricated systems that are designed specifically for cable rails. These systems can vary widely from the ultra modern to the fairly pedestrian.

The other option to consider is whether to run the cables horizontally or vertically. Horizontal cables are the more traditional application, but there is nothing in the code that says they can't run vertically (or diagonally for that matter). If you choose to run the cables vertically, consider using a metal rails that can resist the considerable force exerted by the tight cables.

NONWOOD RAILINGS (CONTINUED)

Vinyl and other plastics

Vinyl is used for many home-construction elements from small parts in appliances to most famously as siding. Vinyl railing systems usually incorporate metal or wood for structure. They boast elegant and upscale profiles that require little more than snap-together skills for installation. Manufacturers note that maintenance is very light for long-lasting good looks and a durable product.

Plastic options on the market include urethane, fiberglass, and cellular PVC. The basic selling point is good looks with low maintenance. The reality is that the quality does not depend on the material but on the company that manufactures the product. When researching, be thorough. Talk to customers who've installed and lived with the product for at least a year or more. Also a quick Internet search will usually turn up a raft of comments, justified or not.

Vinyl needs to be supported **with wood or metal inside the posts and rails.**

WORKING WITH KITS

Working with railing kits can be a blessing or the bane of your deck-building experience. Railing kits can often provide a look that is hard (or nearly impossible) to obtain by fabricating the parts yourself. However, the ease with which the systems are assembled can vary tremendously. The key consideration is whether the kit allows for custom spacing between balusters and posts. Some systems require specific spacing, which needs to be considered when you are designing your deck.

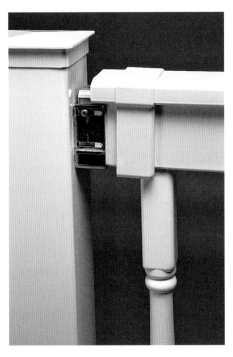

With any vinyl system, you'll need to have a toolbox handy to secure the mechanical connectors that hold the assembly together.

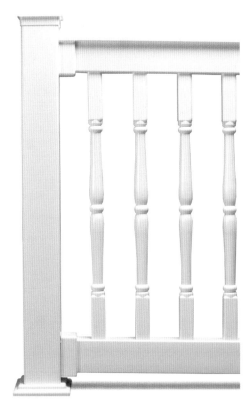

Composite systems

For people who like composite wood decking for its environmentally friendly attributes, looks, or durability, there is no reason not also to like the railing parts that are manufactured to match. Composite railing systems are typically manufactured from a blend of new and recycled plastic and wood as well as adhesives. They come in a wide variety of colors and finishes, ranging from products that are nearly indistinguishable from wood at first glance to those that have a PVC coating that successfully mimics a high-quality painted finish.

Metal and other materials

You have a wide choice in metal railing styles, from the look of a gothic roof railing to the utilitarian railing of a hotel pool deck. Metal per pound is stronger than either wood or composite, so the balusters can be thinner with the same strength. Metal railings are obviously extremely durable, but ferrous metals can and will rust without a proper coating, especially in marine zones. Recently, strong glass products have become more readily available and can be used between extruded metal posts for an ultra-modern railing system. Metal parts like balusters can be used with traditional wood systems to add variety and a custom look.

Composites behave much like lumber **when cutting and fastening so for many people there is a ready-made sense of comfort when working with the material.**

A metal support system allows a transparent panel to fit in a groove as a replacement for traditional balusters.

High-end railing systems **are not necessarily easier to assemble but generally have better detailing for a more refined look.**

INSTALLING THE NEWEL POSTS

The tensioner hardware **transfers any load applied to the newel post to the joist and decking assembly.**

1 Start with post stock that is longer than you need.

2 Mark the newel post, then measure down to the first bolt hole.

3 Mark the center locations of the holes using a Speed Square.

The most readily available railing system is one that you build on site. You can either use parts purchased at the local lumberyard or fabricate some of the parts yourself. The railing assembly process outlined here uses a combination of hardwood balusters that match the decking material and cedar rails, posts, and custom cap.

The first step in building the railing is to install the newel posts. Newel post installation uses the same lateral-tension hardware as for connecting the joist assembly to the house framing (see "Installing the Ledger" on p. 106). The hardware relies on a bolt passing through the post and rim for half of the connection. The other half of the connection is secured to blocking or the joist framing. The easiest way to align the hardware bolts with both the posts and the deck framing is to start by boring the newel post and working back to the framing.

Preparing the newel post

To prepare the post, start with post stock that is longer than you need for an overall height **1**. Once you've installed the railings, you can cut all the posts to the same height. Begin by laying out the bolt locations. Mark the top of the rim on the newel post and then measure down to the top bolt **2**. Measure down to the bottom bolt in the same manner

and align the bolt locations in the center with a Speed Square **3**. The bolt holes are typically located 2 in. down from the decking and 2 in. up from the post bottom, flush with the framing.

Use a boring bit with a self-tapping tip to drill the bolt holes. A typical drill bit will have a tendency to wander, so start the hole with an awl for the best results **4**, **5**. Care-

4 Align an awl to the bolt-hole center mark and make a starting depression to guide the bit location.

5 Use a boring bit to drill the hole—the self-tapping tip will guide the bit better.

6 Bore the hole halfway though the post from both sides.

7 Ream the hole straight so the bolt shank can pass through the post easily.

8 Test-fit a bolt to make sure it will pass through the hole easily.

fully align the drill plumb to the hole and bore both holes halfway through **6**. Once the holes meet, ream out the center to allow the bolt shaft to pass through easily **7**. However, be careful not to enlarge the holes at the post face. The last step in preparing the post before install is to test-fit a bolt **8**.

TRADE SECRET

Lay out the posts by establishing the corner-post location and then equally dividing the space in between into sections that are typically between 5 ft. and 7 ft. To account for post thickness, reference the calculations from the post centers.

INSTALLING THE NEWEL POSTS (CONTINUED)

Securing the newel post

Locate the newel according to the deck plans and clamp a scrap block of framing lumber under the center of the rim joist to act as a third hand ❶. Set the newel post in place on the third-hand block and clamp it against the rim joist ❷. Adjust the post to plumb ❸ and temporarily secure it with screws driven through the rim joist ❹. Using the predrilled hole in the post as a guide, bore through the rim joist at both the top and the bottom bolt locations ❺. Pass a bolt through the top hole and slide the tensioner plate onto the bolt ❻. Secure the rim to the post with a bolt through the bottom hole as well ❼ (p. 172). The bottom bolt doesn't need a tensioner.

Cut and fit a section of blocking between the rim and the adjacent joist ❽ (p. 172). You'll want to make sure that the blocking sits square to the joist, the tensioner plate sits flat against the block, and the end seats to both the joist and the block ❾ (p. 172). This ensures that the loads placed on the post will be properly transferred into the joist system.

Flush the blocking to the joist tops and secure it with 3-in. through screws ❿ (p. 172). The beefy fasteners for the tensioner plate require a predrill to ensure that the short length of blocking doesn't split ⓫ (p. 173). After drilling each hole location, drive the hex-head fasteners that are specified by the manufacturer ⓬ (p. 173).

The next step is to install the opposing tensioner in essentially the same fashion. To align the hole location, hold the tensioner in place and mark where the bolt passes through the plate at the end ⓭ (p. 173). After boring the hole, secure the bolt and then attach the plate fasteners, as you did before ⓮ (p. 173).

1 Clamp a scrap of framing lumber under the post location to support the weight of the post.

2 Clamp the post to the rim joist once the post is positioned on the support block at the layout location.

3 Plumb the post using a level, double-checking to make sure the post doesn't move off layout.

4 Secure the post temporarily with 3-in. screws. Be sure to stay clear of the bolt-hole locations.

5 Bore through the rim joist using the hole in the post as a guide.

6 Slip the tensioner hardware on the bolt shank and hand-tighten the bolt.

INSTALLING THE NEWEL POSTS (CONTINUED)

7 Align and install the second bolt without a tensioner to secure the bottom of the post to the rim joist.

8 Position blocking between the rim joist and the adjacent joist.

9 Align the blocking so the tension plate sits flush to both the rim and the blocking.

10 Flush the top of the blocking with the joist and secure the blocking with 3-in. screws.

⚠ WHAT CAN GO WRONG

If you bore straight through the post, chances are the bit will wander off center by the time it gets all the way through. To keep the hole true, mark the layout on opposite faces of the post and bore halfway from each side. When the holes meet ream them straight.

11 Drill pilot holes at each fastener hole provided for in the tensioner plate.

12 Drive the manufacturer-specified fastener through each hole in the plate to secure the hardware.

13 Mark the bolt hole through the adjacent joist by holding the hardware in position against the blocking.

14 Secure the second tensioner plate in the same manner as the first.

TRADE SECRET

Technically, lateral load hardware is not required by code but the protection it provides is. If your framing configuration doesn't work with the lateral-load tensioner in the process shown here, you can provide the same protection by blocking around the post with framing. The challenge will be in getting the building department and the inspector to agree.

BUILDING AND INSTALLING A SITE-BUILT BALUSTRADE

1 Measure up from the finished deck to the underside of the railing cap.

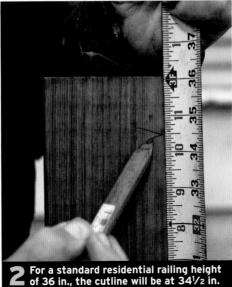

2 For a standard residential railing height of 36 in., the cutline will be at 34½ in.

3 Level between the posts to transfer the cutline elevation to all the posts.

4 Draw the cutline all the way around each post to provide a good reference for the cut.

5 Cut all the posts to the same height. For reference, sight down the line of posts to check that they are all the same height.

Of all the railing options, installing a site-built railing will probably get you the most bang for your buck without the hassle of product research, ordering, and an installation learning curve. The balustrade installation outlined here uses off-the-shelf hardwood balusters chosen because they match the decking but also because they have a slightly smaller profile than a typi-cal softwood baluster. The rails are made of cedar 1× lumber, ripped on site, to match the cedar posts and custom cap.

Cutting the posts and rails

It's important to cut all the posts at an even height so the finished cap doesn't wander up and down. To avoid transferring discrepancies from the decking to the railing, establish the height of one post and then transfer that elevation to the other posts. First, measure up from the finished deck height to the location of the underside of the railing to establish the top of the posts ❶. For a 36-in. railing height with a 2×6 cap, the cutline will be 34½ in. ❷. Level between the posts to transfer that elevation to all the posts ❸. With a Speed Square, continue the elevation

6 Mark the distance between two posts on a length of rail. This will become a story pole on which to mark the baluster locations.

7 Cut four rail pieces to that length and test-fit them between the posts.

8 Test-fit two of the rail pieces between the posts at the height of installation.

9 Identify where the railing pieces go by writing their location on the back after you've fit them.

line all the way around each post to ensure a continuous guide for the sawblade **4**. Cut all the posts to the same height. A good check is to eye down the tops of the posts to make sure they are all aligned **5**.

To determine the rail length, place a 1× between the posts at the bottom and mark the length **6**. For the deck shown here, there is a pair of rails for the bottom and a pair for the top (inside and outside for each). If you've been careful to keep everything plumb, the distance between the posts shouldn't differ from the top and bottom. If the distance is within an 1/8 in. or so, just treat the measurements as identical and cut all four rails the same length; test-fit them at the bottom **7**. Sometimes post distance will vary a little from top to bottom, and it's more

work than it's worth to adjust them. In these cases, treat the bottom and top separately and fit them as pairs of railings **8**. Identify the show face (the better-looking side) and label the rails on the back to indicate where they go **9**.

BUILDING AND INSTALLING A SITE-BUILT BALUSTRADE (CONTINUED)

Use a guide for a perfect cut

If you're not confident about freehanding a straight cut, it takes only a minute to set up a guide that will ensure a perfect cut every time.

Measure the distance from the side of the blade to the edge of the saw base ❶. This is the blade offset. Measure the distance of the offset down from the elevation line and make a mark ❷. Square the mark across the face of the post and around all four sides ❸. Clamp a guide board aligned to the lower line ❹. Use the block to guide the saw. After the first cut, reposition the block on the opposite face to finish the cut ❺.

Establishing baluster spacing

Calculating the baluster spacing is not difficult, but it does require a little back and forth. Unless the spacing between all the posts is perfectly uniform, it's best to calculate the baluster spacing for each run separately. Typically, your eye will not pick up small differences in spacing from one run to the next but will immediately identify one space that is not the same as the rest in the run. To calculate the spacing, begin by measuring the distance between the posts **①**. To keep the measurements straight and to avoid error, it's best to have a calculation sheet to write the measurements down on (see "Calculating the Baluster Spacing" below). To the distance between the posts add one baluster thickness **②**.

> ➡ See "Railings are assemblies of posts, rails, caps, and balusters," p. 164.

The maximum distance allowed between balusters by code is 4 in., so set two balusters down with a 4-in. gap between them and measure the space between the balusters plus one baluster thickness **③**. This is the estimated baluster-unit distance. Now divide the overall distance by the unit distance to determine the number of units. In this case, the number is about 7½ **④**. Round up to the next whole number and divide it back into the overall distance to get the final baluster-unit distance. In this case the baluster-unit distance is just over 5 in **⑤**.

1 Measure the distance between two posts to begin calculating the baluster spacing.

2 Add the width of one baluster to the post spacing to get the overall distance.

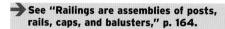

3 Calculate the baluster-unit distance by adding 4 in. to the width of one baluster.

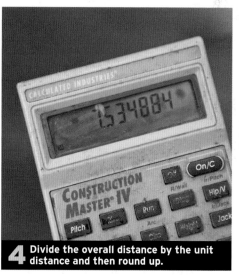

4 Divide the overall distance by the unit distance and then round up.

5 Divide the number of spaces back into the overall distance.

CALCULATING THE BALUSTER SPACING

- Distance between posts + One baluster thickness = Overall balustrade distance ÷ estimated baluster-unit distance = Number of units fraction
- Round number of units up to the next whole number = Final number of baluster units
- Overall balustrade distance ÷ Final baluster units = Final baluster-unit distance

Note that the final baluster-unit distance is what you use to lay out the balusters, but if you want to check the exact distance between the balusters, simply subtract the baluster thickness from the final baluster-unit distance.

BUILDING AND INSTALLING A SITE-BUILT BALUSTRADE (CONTINUED)

1 Clamp the story pole to the rails of a section positioned between the posts.

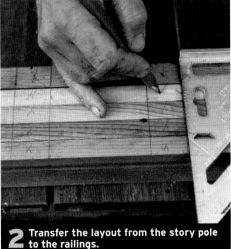

2 Transfer the layout from the story pole to the railings.

3 Continue the layout marks down the insides of the rails.

4 Place a spacer no more than 4 in. tall at the base of the post.

5 Measure from the spacer to the top of the post to establish the baluster height.

6 Assemble the rails and balusters on the deck adjacent to their final position.

7 Position the opposing rail on top of the balusters. Take care to orient the rails appropriately.

Assembling and securing the balustrade

To increase efficiency and avoid mistakes, make a story pole of baluster spacing and clamp it in place with the actual balusters **1**. Transfer the baluster layout to the rails, making an X for each baluster **2**. Unclamp the rails and transfer the layout up the rails' inside faces **3**. By code, the maximum allowable gap between the decking and the rail bottom is also 4 in. To establish the correct baluster length, place a 4-in. (or less) spacer on the deck **4**. Measure to the top of the post for the overall baluster length **5**. Cut

8 Mark the fastener locations with a gauge to ensure that they are uniform. A slight depression from the awl will help guide the bit.

9 Flush the rails and balusters with a Speed Square before drilling the pilot holes.

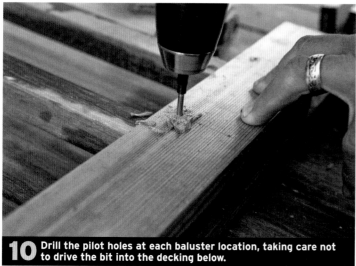

10 Drill the pilot holes at each baluster location, taking care not to drive the bit into the decking below.

11 Drive a fastener into each hole to secure the rails and balusters.

all the balusters and place them according to the layout on a top and bottom rail on the deck surface **6**. Place the other top and bottom rails over the balusters, being careful to align the ends and the layout marks **7**. To create a uniform assembly, mark the fastener location with a stop or marking jig at every baluster location **8**. As it's easy for the individual boards to shift before they are secure, use a square to flush the baluster bottoms and rail edges before predrilling the holes **9**. Hold the assembly firmly while predrilling the holes **10**. Check the assembly again for alignment and then drive the fasteners to secure the bottom part of the balustrade **11**.

Setting up a chop-saw cut station

A mini-version of the cut station shown on p. 154 will make quick work of cutting the balusters. To set up the station, screw or clamp a board flat on the chopsaw base.

Measure over from the blade and attach a stop square to the blade **1**. When you make the first cut, the base will be cut to length along with any balusters in the rig **2**.

BUILDING AND INSTALLING A SITE-BUILT BALUSTRADE (CONTINUED)

12 Position the top rail adjacent to the bottom rail and transfer the baluster locations, again making a dimple with your awl.

13 Repeat the process of aligning and securing the rails to the balusters at the top of the assembly.

14 Test-fit the baluster and make any adjustments necessary to achieve a snug fit.

15 Fasten short lengths of baluster material to the posts between where the rails intersect the posts.

16 Angle the top of the blocks where they are exposed to the weather. This will help shed water and prevent rot.

TRADE SECRET

Keep a trim router fitted with a small roundover bit handy. As you finish each section, quickly give the sharp edges a pass to remove splinters and give the balustrade a more finished look.

17 Slide the balustrade in from the side just above where the rails intersect the blocks.

18 Slide the balustrades down into position so that all four blocks are hidden behind the rails.

19 Flush the top of the rail with the top of the posts. Double-check to make sure the balustrade is aligned the way you want it.

20 Secure the balustrade with fasteners at each of the four blocks.

Rather than measuring for the fastener locations in the top rail, align the top rail next to the bottom rail you just secured and transfer the fastener locations with a Speed Square **12**. Repeat the process of drilling pilot holes and driving fasteners to secure the balusters and top rails **13**. Test-fit the assembled balustrade to make sure it fits properly before attaching it permanently **14**.

To secure the balustrade at the top, first cut a short section of baluster and fasten it to the post in the center **15**. At the bottom, cut the top of the block at an angle to shed water and prevent rot, and then attach it where the bottom rail meets the post **16**. Slide the rail in from the side just above the

blocks **17** and then guide it down into place **18**. Flush the top of the rail to the post top **19**. If everything fits, you shouldn't have to do more than some gentle tapping to persuade it into position. Finally, use fasteners to secure the rails to the blocks **20**. Be careful with this process because the short blocks tend to split if you overdrive the fasteners or neglect to drill fastener pilot holes.

WHAT CAN GO WRONG

Don't damage the decking. Check the predrill bit to make sure you know when to stop before boring into the new decking.

INSTALLING THE RAILING CAP

A railing cap installation is a fairly straightforward process. For the cap shown here, we used a typical top-down fastener. The challenge for this installation was at the corners. Because we beveled the top, the corner joint needed to be mitered. To make a mitered joint in the cap, first set the outside overhang, in this case 1 in. ❶. Measure one length of the cap and add the overhang to get the distance to the long point of the miter ❷. For example, if the cap length is 41⅛ in. and the overhang is 1 in., make the piece 42⅛ in. from one end to the long point of the miter ❸. Before installing the cap, round over any sharp edges with the trim router ❹. Cut both legs of the cap and then fit the miter first ❺. To secure the miter, drive a 3½-in. screw from the side ❻. After the miter is set, secure the rest of the cap rail with top-down screws into the posts ❼.

1 Measure the outside overhang to begin the miter calculation.

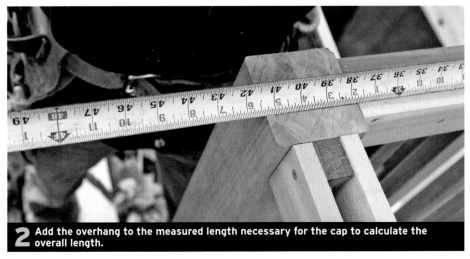

2 Add the overhang to the measured length necessary for the cap to calculate the overall length.

Secure the railing cap from the top with pan-head fasteners. **To avoid splitting the cap, drill a pilot hole through the cap that is the same size as the fastener shank.**

MAKE A CUSTOM RAILING CAP

Trying to buy railing cap can be frustrating. Often what you find is expensive or of poor quality, and if you do find something you like, it's often on back order. Fortunately, if you have a typical bench planer, a simple jig lets you make a custom railing cap out of standard 2× decking stock.

The jig consists of an auxiliary base of white shelving stock, a guide stop to hold the cap stock in place (seen here on the right fastened to the top of the auxiliary base), and a lift block to raise the auxiliary base to sit at an angle. To fashion the cap, simply plane the board to the centerline oriented from both directions.

3 Cut the cap at a 45° miter using the overall cap length and measuring from the long point.

4 Round over any sharp edges to prevent injury and help the cap last longer.

5 Fit the miter, paying close attention to the overhang along the cap's length.

6 Secure the miter with a fastener driven across the joint. If you like, you can also use all-weather glue in the joint.

7 Overhang the post with the cap by several inches where you will add a stair railing.

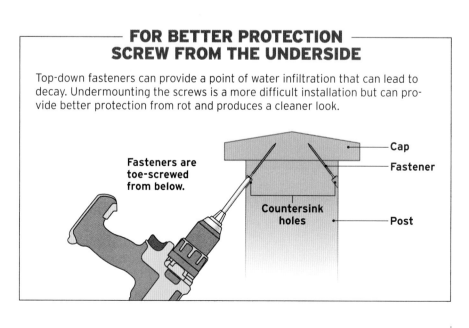

FOR BETTER PROTECTION
SCREW FROM THE UNDERSIDE

Top-down fasteners can provide a point of water infiltration that can lead to decay. Undermounting the screws is a more difficult installation but can provide better protection from rot and produces a cleaner look.

Fasteners are toe-screwed from below.

Cap

Fastener

Countersink holes

Post

ESTABLISHING MEASUREMENTS AND REFERENCE LINES

1 Align the section of rail along the tops of the tread nosings to establish the angle.

2 Mark the angle and length on the end of the rail where it intersects the post face.

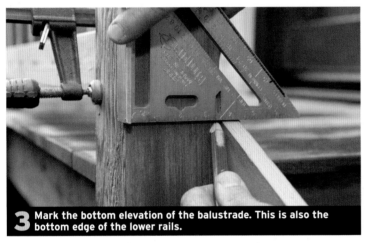

3 Mark the bottom elevation of the balustrade. This is also the bottom edge of the lower rails.

4 Mark the angle and length on the other end of the rail. Double-check to make sure the rail has not moved while making your marks.

5 Check the rake angle and record it on a piece of paper.

The challenge to installing a handrail on a stair is that you can't just level over or easily measure up. However, by using the stair tread's nosings as a point of reference, the installation is not much more difficult than for a typical railing.

Start by aligning a lower-rail section on top of the stair nosings and clamping it in place **1**. Mark the cutline on the lower rail where it intersects the upper post **2**. Also mark the bottom of the balustrade assembly by aligning a square across the post face where it intersects the top edge of the rail **3**. Repeat this process of marking the rail cutline and the bottom of the balustrade where the rail intersects with the post at the bottom of the stair run **4**.

FROM THE BOTTOM UP

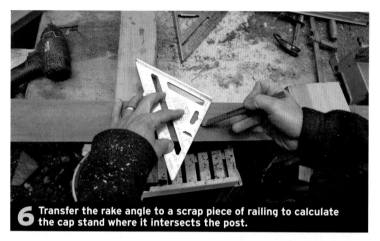

6 Transfer the rake angle to a scrap piece of railing to calculate the cap stand where it intersects the post.

7 Align a section of cap with the bottom flush to the edge of the rail and the rake line intersecting the cap apex.

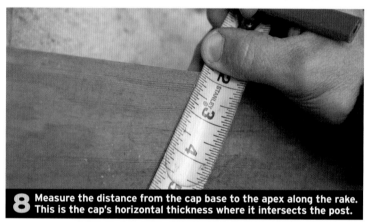

8 Measure the distance from the cap base to the apex along the rake. This is the cap's horizontal thickness where it intersects the post.

9 Measure down from underneath the horizontal cap the distance you just measured as the cap's stand.

10 Mark a horizontal line across the post face that represents the underside of the cap on the rake.

11 Measure the distance between the two lines you have made on the post face to establish the overall height of the balustrade.

Next you'll want to cut the post to height at the rake. With the lower section of rail still clamped in place against the tread nosings, take a reading of the rake angle with a Speed Square **5**. Transfer that angle to a scrap board so you can record the vertical stand of the cap **6**. To do this, position a section of cap on the angle you just made with the cap apex intersecting the rake angle **7**. Measure the distance along the rake angle from the base of the cap to the apex. This is the cap's vertical stand where it intersects the post **8**. Now measure down from the underside of the typical railing cap **9**. This represents the intersection of the underside of the cap and the post. Use a Speed Square to carry this line across the post face **10**. Measure between the two lines

ESTABLISHING MEASUREMENTS AND REFERENCE LINES FROM THE

12 Measure up the distance of the overall balustrade registered on the mark you made on the inside face of the lower post.

13 Mark the top of the balustrade on the inside face of the post.

14 Extend the line across the face that represents where the underside of the cap will intersect the post.

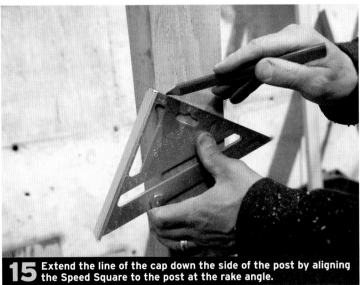

15 Extend the line of the cap down the side of the post by aligning the Speed Square to the post at the rake angle.

drawn on the post face to establish the baluster length from long point to short point **11** (p. 185).

Transfer the baluster length (also the balustrade height) to the bottom post to locate where to cut the top of the post. To do this, measure from the bottom line already drawn on the post face **12**. Measure up the distance of the baluster length and make a mark **13**. With a Speed Square, extend this line across the post face **14**. On the side faces, extend

the line at the rake angle **15**. Cut the top of the post at the rake angle **16**.

To fit a cap to the rake railing section, cut one end of a cap section (at least 12 in. longer than you need) at the rake angle and fit it in position at the upper post **17**. At the bottom post, plumb a level 2 in. or so down the rake **18**. Using the level as reference, mark the plumb line on the cap **19**. At this point, you can set the cap aside until you are ready to install it.

BOTTOM UP (CONTINUED)

16 Cut the post at the rake angle, using the lines you just drew as reference.

17 Fit a section of cap to the post with the end cut plumb to the complement of the rake angle.

18 Mark the plumb end cut on the cap a couple inches down the rake from the lower post.

19 Use a level to mark this cut. Then remove the cap and cut it from the underside and set it aside until you are ready to install it.

ASSEMBLING THE RAILING IN PLACE

Unlike assembling the balustrades for the typical railing sections, balustrades for the stair are assembled
in place. Begin the assembly by cutting the lower section
of rail and test-fitting it in place ❶. Do the same with the
upper section, and while you're at it locate the attachment blocks ❷. Just as with the typical railing, the
attachment block is a short section of balustrade cut at
the rake angle ❸. Attach the upper and lower rails to
the blocks on the posts before beginning the baluster
installation.

To install the balusters, make a story pole in the same
way as for the typical railing sections and then clamp
it level between the posts ❹. Use a framing square to
align the railing plumb and to the layout ❺. Secure the
cap with top-down fasteners driven into the post ❻. The
heads of these fasteners sit below the cap surface, so
for added protection against rot, consider countersink-
ing and plugging the holes.

1 Cut and test-fit all four rail sections before attempting to install
any of them.

2 Align the attachment blocks using the rail as a guide.

3 Double-check the block position referenced to the cap lines
you have drawn on the post face.

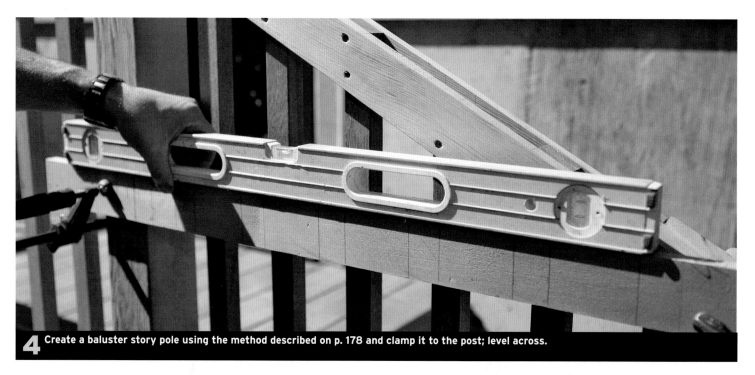

4 Create a baluster story pole using the method described on p. 178 and clamp it to the post; level across.

5 Align the balusters with a framing square (note that in this photo all the balusters shown have already been installed).

6 Secure the cap with top-down fasteners driven into the top of the post.

DECK STAIRS

MOST DECK PROJECTS HAVE some stairs that need to be built. Even a grade-level deck often has one or two steps that access the surrounding grade from the deck. No matter how many steps a deck needs or the manner of construction, the underlying principles are the same and have been refined by stair builders for centuries. Today, these techniques are written into the modern stair-building code.

While building stairs is the most advanced aspect of deck construction, if you are armed with the right layout tools, the math becomes manageable and the carpentry itself is no more difficult than the framing and decking for the rest of the project. In this chapter, you'll learn all the steps of how to install a short run of stairs, including techniques for calculating stair height and tread depth, securing stringers, and installing treads.

GENERAL PREPARATION

The Basics of Stair Building, p. 192

PREPARING THE STRINGERS

INSTALLING STRINGERS

INSTALLING TREADS AND RISERS

THE BASICS OF STAIR BUILDING

Even for people who don't like math, stair building can be a manageable and rewarding part of building a deck. The best way to prepare is to break down the challenge into smaller units and plan out each unit before buying materials or breaking out the tools. The basic phases are taking measurements, designing a plan, buying materials, and installation. Taking the initial measurements is crucial and often involves extending level lines without solid reference points. If you can find reliable help but only for one day, have them help with the measuring part rather than the installation.

Designing a stair plan is great practice for installation so resist the urge to launch yourself into the installation before you have a complete drawing with all the calculated measurements filled in. One quirk to designing stairs is that the calculations involve dividing fractions on a 1/16-in. scale. There are calculators to handle this for you but they can be pricey. Fortunately, if you already own a smart phone there are numerous free apps that are designed for construction calculations in English units.

Stair building combines all the phases of deck building from foundation through railing installation into one project. Likewise, the material list will be just as varied. When writing a shopping list, it's helpful to organize the materials by type (foundation, framing, railing, etc.).

Building stairs requires you to think in 3D spaces and is the most challenging aspect of deck building. However, approached with an organized plan, this can be rewarding project for any deck builder.

WHAT YOU'LL NEED

FOUNDATION
- 4 bags of Quikrete®
- 1 stick of rebar
- 1/2 yd. of gravel
- Two 2×8-in. by 8-ft. form boards
- Twisty ties for rebar

FRAMING
- Four 2×8-in. by 8-ft. pieces of pressure-treated stringer stock
- Two 2×4-in. by 8-ft. pieces of pressure-treated stock for strongbacks
- 4 stringer hangers
- Angle brackets for attachment to grade beam
- Fasteners

DECKING
- Two 4-ft. pieces of decking stock for every stair
- Fasteners

RAILING
- Two 6-ft. posts
- Four 8-ft. boards for rail material
- Two 8-ft. pieces of cap stock
- Three 36-in. pieces of baluster stock for every linear foot of railing

Rise and run

Rise and run are two essential terms to know when discussing stair design and construction. The rise is the distance each step goes up and the run is the horizontal distance between steps. If we look at a drawing of a stair plan, we notice that there's also a total rise, which is the elevation change from the grade at the bottom of the stairs to the top of the decking. Likewise, the total run is the horizontal distance between the beginning and end of the stairs. These distances are measured from very specific stair-framing elements.

ALL STAIRS HAVE THE SAME BASIC ELEMENTS

No matter the details of your project, your stairs will have some universal features. Once you identify those features for your stairs and take the measurements, you can follow a well-established protocol to guide you through cutting and installing the parts.

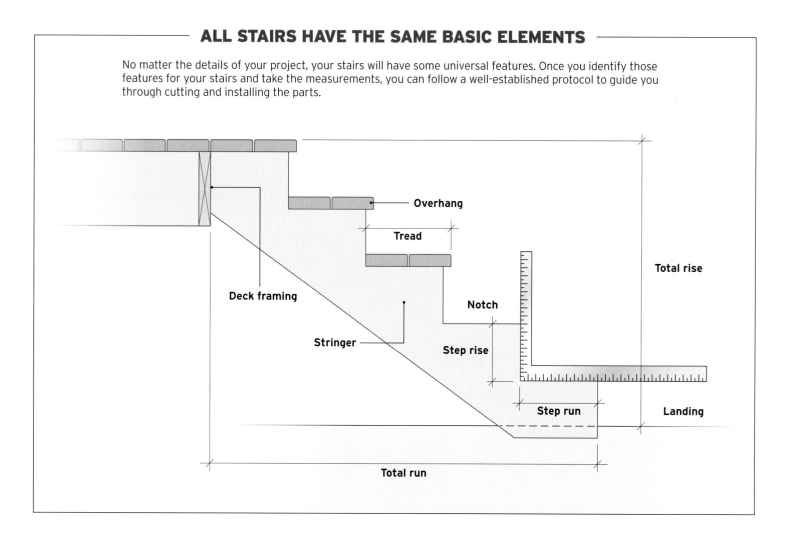

STRINGER LAYOUT

Decks built for the vast majority of homes will need a few steps to connect the deck to the surrounding yard. For these projects, a basic set of stairs as shown here will work well.

Once you've located where the stairs will attach to the deck framing according to the plans, you can measure for the rise and run. First, measure for the rise by establishing a level line from the top of the decking at the attachment point ❶. On this project, the stairs were adjacent to the foundation wall, which was a handy place to mark the stair geometry. For situations that don't have this convenience, mark the measurements down on a drawing. Using the level, mark a horizontal line near where the stairs will land ❷. Then measure down from the level line to the top of grade ❸. While this sounds pretty simple, knowing exactly where to measure the grade requires knowing exactly how the stringers will be supported.

If the landscaping is still rough, you can establish the stair-landing elevation by referencing the surrounding grade. You'll want to raise the stair landing slightly to avoid water pooling at the bottom of the stairs.

➡ See "Installing a Grade Beam," p. 83.

Once you know the distance from the top of the decking to the stair landing, divide the distance by the estimated number of risers: Total rise ÷ Number of stairs = Individual stair rise.

If you are lucky, the calculation for the individual stair rise will be around 7 in. If the calculation is less than 6 in. or more than 8 in., try adding or subtracting a step accordingly, then recalculate the step rise.

Making minor adjustments to rise and run will change the "mood" of the stairs. For relaxed stairs, lengthen the run and shorten the rise. For more aggressive stairs (that is, steeper stairs), shorten the run and raise the rise. While code will vary a little, generally you'll want to keep the rise between 4 in. and 7½ in. and keep the run over 10 in.

1 Level across from the finished deck height. If the decking is not installed (as here), place a scrap of decking on top of the framing to establish the correct height.

2 Mark the deck elevation over the stair landing location. If you don't have a wall handy, find a helper to hold and read the level.

3 Measure down to the top of grade or stair landing to determine the overall rise.

CUTTING THE STRINGERS

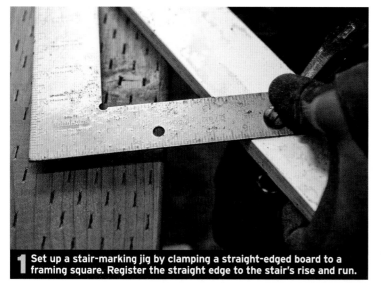

1 Set up a stair-marking jig by clamping a straight-edged board to a framing square. Register the straight edge to the stair's rise and run.

2 Mark the first stair notch in the stringer. Orient this notch at least 12 in. from the board's end and clear of any knots.

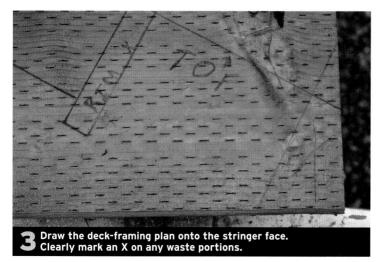

3 Draw the deck-framing plan onto the stringer face. Clearly mark an X on any waste portions.

4 Align a Speed Square to the adjacent notch line to increase the accuracy of stringer layout.

With the rise and run calculated, you can set up a framing square to mark out the stair notches on the stringer. Clamp a straight length of scrap wood (leftover trim stock works well) to a framing square, with the wood's edge registered to the rise and run measurements **1**. I've seen some carpenters use spring clamps to hold the straightedge in place, but C-clamps hold the jig setup more securely and thus reduce the chance of a layout error. Place the jig 12 in. or so in from the end, avoiding any knots in the wood that might weaken the stringer.

Draw the first stair notch using the framing square as a guide **2**. Before drawing the rest of the stair notches, draw all of the framing elements where the stringer will attach to the deck framing **3**. This allows you to verify that you've left enough wood at the stringer's top to secure it to the framing and also allows you to verify your stair calculations.

To mark out the rest of the notches, slide the framing square to the next step, referencing the previous notch. There is a chance that you might wander off layout using this method. On short runs this is not a problem, but on longer runs it can be more of a concern. Short of laying the whole stringer out with a construction calculator, you

TRADE SECRET

Make an educated guess for rise and run. Before leveling out to measure the rise, measure down from the decking to the grade and divide the length by 7½ in. If the grade drops only a little, this will give you the number of risers plus or minus one.

CUTTING THE STRINGERS (CONTINUED)

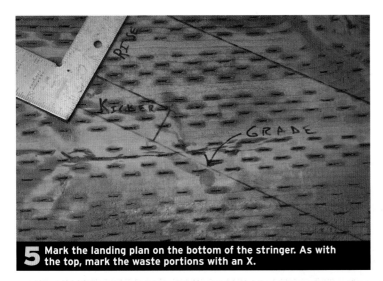

5 Mark the landing plan on the bottom of the stringer. As with the top, mark the waste portions with an X.

6 Cut the notches with a circular saw, being careful not to overcut the line.

7 Finish the notch cut with a handsaw or jigsaw.

8 Cut inside corners carefully with a jigsaw.

9 Apply wood preservative to all fresh cuts.

can increase accuracy by aligning a Speed Square to the adjacent triangle ❹ (p. 195). At the bottom of the run, draw the grade and kicker onto the board as with the top ❺. Cut the notches with a circular saw, being careful not to overcut the inside of the notch ❻. The waste portion of the notch will easily break off at this point.

To clean up the stringer, finish the notch cuts with a handsaw or jigsaw ❼. To avoid overcuts that might weaken the stringer, use a jigsaw where the layout calls for a tight inside corner ❽. To protect the stringer and preserve all the hard work you've just invested, apply a coat of wood preservative to all freshly cut ends ❾.

WHAT CAN GO WRONG

Using stair-gauge nuts on a framing square to mark out the stringer's rise and run is common practice. But using them on notoriously inconsistent pressure-treated lumber can be a problem because it can cause your stairs to vary in height.

TRADE SECRET

Mark the waste sections with an X. While what is waste and what is not may seem obvious while marking the stringer, just a few minutes later when you're focused on making accurate cuts, it easy to forget which side of the line to cut on.

CONNECTING THE STRINGERS TO THE DECK FRAMING

1 Test-fit the stringers before permanently securing them, being careful not to force the stringer into position.

2 Attach the stringer to the framing with temporary screws and register all three stringers from the same attachment point.

3 Check the stringer for a level run. If the run slopes back, the bottom of the stringer needs to drop in relation to the top.

4 Position all three stringers temporarily and repeat checks for overall fit and levelness of the run.

There are three important aspects to installing stringers. First, the connection to the framing at the top of the stringer must be secure and able to support the weight of the stairs plus the considerable weight of additional loads. Second, the stringer must land on a solid base that, like the top, must support the load. In addition, the bottom connection must also resist the tendency of the stairs to kick away from the deck. And third, the geometry of the installation must agree with how the stringers were cut—that is, the run of each step must be level or nearly so.

> **See "Installing a Grade Beam," p. 83**

No matter what attachment method you choose (see "Options for securing stringers" on p. 199), it's a good idea to fit the stringers before permanently securing them **1**. Locate the temporary screw low in the notch to reduce the risk of splitting the stringer before it's permanently attached **2**. With one stringer in place and resting on the landing, check the run for level **3**. If the stringer's run is level or pitched slightly toward the stringer bottom, that's acceptable. If the slope is back, meaning the edge of the step closest to you when you walk up the steps is higher, then adjust the stringer position until the stringer run is level.

Temporarily attach all three stringers in place and double-check that they are located correctly **4**. Often stringers will

CONNECTING THE STRINGERS TO THE DECK FRAMING (CONTINUED)

5 Level across all three stringers. The stringers should be within 1/16 in. If not, adjust the low stringer up if possible.

6 Check the rise alignment of all three stringers at each step and make adjustments so that they are within 1/16 in. at every step.

7 Attach the stringers to the deck framing with screws positioned low on the stringer.

8 Install blocking for joists that do not align with a deck joist. Secure the blocking with through screws or hardware.

have slight variations. To account for this, level across all the stringers at the top step and adjust the middle stringer until it is even with the outside stringers **5**. Level across the stringers at the bottom and adjust the low stringer up with shims until all three stringers are level. Also check the rise face across the stringers to make sure that they

are aligned and make any adjustment necessary **6**. When the stringers are positioned properly, permanently secure them to the deck framing **7**.

For the project shown here, the joists ran parallel to the stringers, so the simplest attachment method was to run the stringer long and sister it to the joist. Whatever

attachment method you choose, it is crucial that the fasteners or hangers secure the stringer near the bottom edge. Any portion of the stringer on the teeth side has no strength. To secure a stringer that does not align with a joist, install blocking to header off the joist end **8**. Then secure the stringer to the blocking with through screws **9**.

9 Screw through the blocking to secure the joist. Fasteners positioned low on the stringer will carry more load.

TRADE SECRET
A strongback is a 2×4 board screwed to the side of the stringer. No matter how short the stair run, strongbacks are necessary to ensure the stringer won't flex or fail with heavy loads.

Options for securing stringers

How you choose to attach the stringer to the deck framing will depend on your preference and on the project details. Shown here are three popular ways to secure stair stringers. One is to lag the butt ends of the stringer directly to the deck rim. This method extends the deck surface over the stringers. A second method is to add a supplemental ledger below the deck framing and support that ledger with posts. This method has the advantage of not putting additional load on the deck framing and is a good choice for a long run of stairs. The third choice is to extend the stringers beyond the ledger and attach them directly to the deck joists. This is a straightforward and secure way to attach stringers.

THREE WAYS TO SECURE STRINGERS

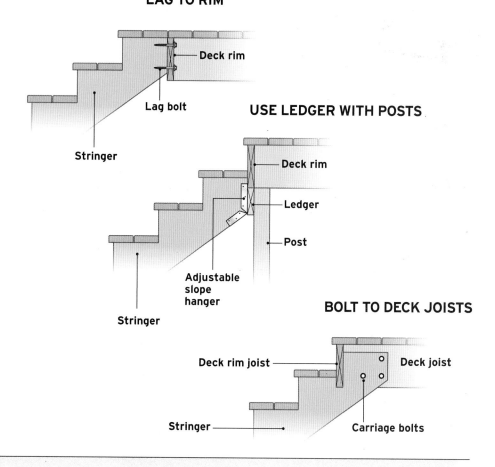

LAG TO RIM

Deck rim
Lag bolt
Stringer

USE LEDGER WITH POSTS

Deck rim
Ledger
Post
Adjustable slope hanger
Stringer

BOLT TO DECK JOISTS

Deck rim joist
Deck joist
Stringer
Carriage bolts

SECURING STRINGERS TO THE LANDING

1 Fit the kicker board into the notches at the bottom of the stringer and then check for level across the stringers.

2 Drill a hole through the kicker board and into the concrete with an appropriately sized masonry bit.

3 Drive a masonry fastener into the concrete to secure the kicker board.

4 Secure the stringer bottom to the kicker with toe screws, being careful not to split the stringer end.

The easiest way to secure the stringers to the landing is with a kicker board. The kicker board is typically located on the landing at the front of the bottom step. Before securing the kicker, check the fit in the kicker recess **1**. With the stringer positioned, use a masonry bit to drill through the kicker into the concrete pad **2**. Then use an appropriately sized masonry bit to fasten the kicker to the pad **3**. The position of the kicker does most of the work by preventing the stringer from moving forward. The connection of the stringer to the kicker is primarily to keep the stair assembly from bouncing or moving side to side, so using screws to fasten the stringer is sufficient **4**. To reduce the chance of splitting the stringer drill a pilot hole for this connection.

OPTIONS FOR SECURING THE STRINGERS TO THE LANDING

It's important to land the stairs on a secure pad that will resist lateral movement. There are three main ways to secure the stringer to the pad to transfer that load. One way is to use galvanized brackets secured to both the stringer and the concrete. This has the advantage that no modifications need to be made when pouring the concrete pad or cutting the stringers. Another method is to secure a pressure-treated kicker board to the pad with masonry bolts. This is a very secure connection because the force of the stringer load pushes directly on the kicker's face. Finally, in drier climates that are less prone to rot, you can choose to embed the kickers in the concrete and secure the stringers with brackets. This method avoids the need for using masonry fasteners.

TWO WAYS TO LAND STRINGERS

WITH HARDWARE

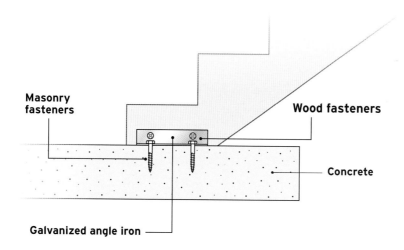

Masonry fasteners

Wood fasteners

Concrete

Galvanized angle iron

WITH A SURFACE KICKER

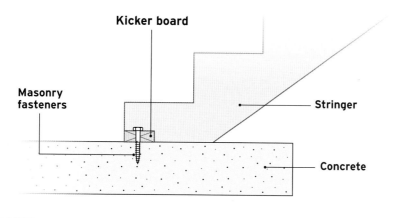

Kicker board

Masonry fasteners

Stringer

Concrete

SECURING THE TREADS

There are a variety of ways to pattern the treads to make them wide enough for comfortable deck stairs. Adding a filler strip in the middle is both decorative and functional.

Wood plugs take a little extra work to install but effectively conceal fasteners. The key to success is ensuring you have a sharp Forstner bit to bore the countersink holes.

Installing treads is much like installing decking. Although with the stair treads, depending on the project details, you may have to decide on a tread pattern. Typical decking is 5½ in. wide, but combining two boards is still a little narrow for a comfortable tread depth, especially when considering the overhang at the tread nosing. For wood decking, adding a 1-in. to 2-in. filler strip between the treads easily solves this issue.

For composite decking, the solution can be a little more involved. For example, capstock decking looks different on the inside, so ripping a tread will show an obvious cut line. Similar difficulties arise with textured composite decking and metal decking. Some manufacturers have tread stock that solves this issue. Alternatively, placing the filler strip at the back to hide the cut face is another way to deal with this.

Installing top-down fasteners

The most common way to secure decking on stairs is to face-screw the decking boards. Even if the main portion of the deck is secured with hidden fasteners, top-screwing the stair may still be a good option because hidden fasteners are sometimes difficult to use with stairs. Some composite decking types have tabs that fit over the screw holes to improve the appearance. In hardwood decking, you can hide the screw holes with plugs.

➜ See "Installing Hidden Fasteners," p. 158.

1 Place the nosing tread in position with the correct overhang. Remember to account for the thickness of the riser.

2 Measure the gap between the treads and then subtract two times the standard decking gap to calculate the width of the filler strip.

3 Rip the filler strip to width and round over the cut edges.

4 Position the inside tread with the correct side overhang. Make a mark on the tread where it sits over the stringer's centerline.

Before installing treads with top-down fasteners, first determine the amount of the overhang **1**. Remember to account for the riser thickness when measuring the over-hang. With the overhang set and the inside tread board in position, measure the width of the filler strip **2**. Before installing the filler strip, round over the cut edge to give it a finished look **3**.

To install the treads, align the inside board with the proper overhang by measuring back under the stringer **4**. This distance will vary depending on your construction details.

WHAT CAN GO WRONG

If you secure the deck board at the top of the stair permanently, the nosing overhang will force you to drive the fastener at an angle. Instead, leave the deck board loose so you can move it out of the way and drive the fastener straight down.

SECURING THE TREADS (CONTINUED)

5 Transfer that mark to the other tread pieces. Make sure the ends are aligned when doing this.

6 Mark the fastener spacing on one set of treads before you start drilling to check that the pattern is both functional and pleasing.

7 Rip spacers to the gap dimension. Hardwood spacers are more accurate and efficient than trying to measure the gap.

8 Make a pilot indentation with an awl. This marks the location and also prevents the drill bit from wandering off layout.

Another way to refine the deck's appearance is to carefully line up the visible fasteners. Stack the treads with the ends aligned and transfer a layout mark that represents the stringer's centerline **5**. Before drilling any holes, mark the fastener locations and set up the boards for one tread to check the spacing **6**. Once the distance between tread boards is established, cutting spacers is an easy way to keep the gaps uniform for the entire run of steps **7**.

Align a gauge or Speed Square to the mark made in step 5 and make a slight indent with an awl **8**. In hardwoods, the indent keeps the drill bit from wandering as you begin the hole. Drill the pilot hole using a 2-in-1 bit **9**. Secure the tread boards before moving on to install the adjacent pieces **10**. Align the filler strip with a spacer positioned over the stringer **11** and with a Speed Square to flush the ends **12**.

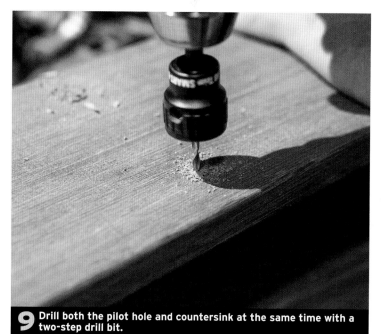

9 Drill both the pilot hole and countersink at the same time with a two-step drill bit.

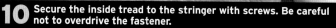

10 Secure the inside tread to the stringer with screws. Be careful not to overdrive the fastener.

11 Position the spacers between the treads to maintain a consistent gap.

12 Flush the tread ends with a square to eliminate any variation of the treads that would detract from the overall appearance.

TRADE SECRET

A 2-in-1 pilot bit will drill a pilot hole and countersink for the head. It also has an adjustable collar to stop the countersink depth where you want it.

SECURING THE TREADS (CONTINUED)

13 Secure the outside tread to the stringer; do not split the stringer.

14 Work up from the bottom when securing treads.

15 Align the ends of the treads with a square to keep a consistent layout.

16 Fit the risers after all the treads have been installed. Orient any gap to the top where it will be hidden by the overhang.

17 Secure the risers using the same layout methods you used with the treads.

Repeat the process to align and secure the outer tread board **13**.

Working from the bottom tread up has the advantage that you have a finished platform to work from **14**. To align the treads from one step to another place a square to reference the upper step with the lower step **15**. After all the treads are installed, fit the risers, leaving any gap hidden under the overhang **16**. Install the risers using the same method of aligning, drilling pilot holes, and securing as you did with the treads **17**.

NOTCH DECKING AROUND NEWELS

Carefully fitting deck boards around newels and other objects will give the deck a professional look. You can do this without using a tape measure; instead, mark the tread in place referencing the side of the post or other obstruction.

1. Place the board you want to notch against the post with the end registered to its final installed position. Using a Speed Square, mark the perpendicular cutline.

2. Use a scrap piece of post material to mark the cut line that will be against the post's forward face.

3. Mark the waste material with an X before moving the board. This will help you avoid the error of cutting to the wrong side of the line. It happens!

4. Use a chopsaw to make the partial perpendicular cut. The blade will not cut completely in the corner but you will finish the cut in the next step.

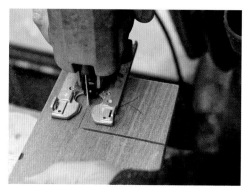

5. Make the adjoining cut with a jigsaw and finish both cuts at the corner.

6. Round the upper edge of the fresh cut with a trim router fitted with the same round-over bit that you used for easing the end cuts.

Test-fit the board and make any adjustments necessary.

DECK
MAINTENANCE

EVERY DECK WILL NEED A BIT OF TLC from time to time. The type of decking and how the owners use the deck are the two main factors that determine how much maintenance any deck will require from year to year. If you want your deck to look new over time, then the amount of maintenance required will be high regardless of the decking material. As a trade-off, plenty of people are fine with their decking starting to age or go gray over time. Of course, letting the decking gray doesn't mean that the deck will be maintenance free. Every deck needs some maintenance.

A maintenance schedule may consist of sealer/UV application, cleaning, fastener tune-up, and replacement of damaged boards. The more organized you are with the care of your deck, the longer it will last and the more you will enjoy it.

WORKING WITH FINISHES

There are many different finishes that can be applied to a deck. Some are sealers that are designed to retard the decking's ability to absorb water. Other finishes go a step further: In addition to sealing the decking, they also provide protection from the damaging effects of UV radiation. This is done by the addition of UV inhibitors to the finish. There is a wide range of protection offered by various finishes on the market. Generally, the greater protection a finish provides the decking, the more the finish will hide the appearance of the decking. Likewise, the clearer the finish, the less UV protection provided and the more often it will need to be applied.

Regardless of which finish is chosen there are a few application rules to follow. Weather will affect how a finish will react with the decking, how well the decking absorbs the finish, and how quickly the finish sets up. The best time to apply a finish is on a day with moderate temperatures. Ideally, there will be no direct sunlight on the target surface, so aim for an overcast day with no rain. Also try to avoid extremes in temperature. For example, don't apply the finish in the evening if the temperature tends to drop after sunset. Keep an eye on the forecast to catch a stretch of weather that will work for you.

Before the staining or sealing starts, give the deck a good cleaning. Now's also a good time to plan on the path you will take when finishing the deck. Generally, work from the inside out and top to bottom. This way you always have an exit plan. You can walk the perimeter while staining the railing and drips are not as catastrophic. As with any finish, work with the grain of the wood. Make sure you are getting enough finish on the decking without applying so much that pooling occurs.

Applying finish with a brush will always work but can be a slow process. A sprayer works well and is much faster but take care not to get finish on plants or the house. When spraying, take the time to protect the surroundings with painter's plastic.

Finishing choices depend on both materials and construction details.

Material choice makes a difference

The choice of decking material you use always determines how much maintenance you will have to do.

Certain softwoods, such as cedar and redwood, have some natural protection against insect and rot damage but will need a yearly scrubbing with brushes and an application of a sealer. If you want to maintain the color, expect to clean and treat the deck at least two or three times a year.

Pressure-treated pine resists rot but will still benefit from a sealer application. It will start out green and eventually go gray. A pigmented sealer will protect the decking from UV rays, something the pressure treating won't, but at a minimum, will require a yearly reapplication.

Exotic hardwoods have a beautiful natural color and resist rot and insects. If you let this deck go gray, you can use a power washer for a yearly cleaning. This option requires the least amount of maintenance of the natural wood material options. As with softwoods, if you want to keep the color, you're facing a sealer application several times a year.

Synthetic decking generally keeps its color well, but be sure to pick a product that has been tested on the market for several years. Decking takes a beating and sometimes manufacturers get it wrong. Depending on the porosity, some synthetic decking will still benefit from yearly sealing.

Stone and metal decking are nearly maintenance free, but you will pay for it in the price up front.

THREE BASIC TYPES OF FINISH

Sealers and stains come in three classes: oil based, water based, and hybrids.

Oil-based finishes have traditionally been used on deck surfaces because of the penetrating quality of the oil, which typically leads to more protection. New synthetic oils tend not to yellow like linseed oil while offering the same protection. However, oil finishes can have high VOCs and require solvents during cleanup.

Water-based finishes carry pigment better than oil finishes for better UV protection, have lower VOC levels, and are easy to clean up. However, the pigment (that is, paint), hides the natural color, grain, and texture of the wood. There are semisolid and semi-transparent choices that show more of the natural wood but also protect it less.

Hybrid finishes have some of the best characteristics of the other types. Like oil, they penetrate into the wood well but, like water-based products, have low VOCs, take pigment well, and clean up with soap and water.

CLEANING IS THE FIRST STEP

A yearly checkup is the minimum maintenance required for a deck. Either spring or fall will work. A spring checkup has the advantage that you can immediately repair any damage from the winter, apply a fresh coat of UV protection, and have your deck looking its best during the main season of use. On the other hand, a fall checkup has the advantage that you are applying sealant protection at the time it will provide the most benefit from the harsh winter conditions. To keep a deck looking its best, plan to do something in both the spring and fall.

In moist climates like the southeast and Pacific Northwest, mold, mildew, and moss can grow quickly on decking. In cold climates, a deck can have dirt and grit from harsh winters as well as residue from de-icing agents. Getting rid of the mold and dirt that has accumulated on the deck can be done with a bristled brush or a pressure washer. If the deck is cedar or pressure treated, then it's best to use deck cleaner and a scrub brush because the wood is softer and is easily damaged by a pressure washer. Some deck cleaners are harmful to plants, so read the label carefully and take necessary precautions.

If the deck is composite or a tropical hardwood, consider using a pressure washer. However, be careful with this machine. While a pressure washer can clean a deck, it can also do a lot of damage. Before cleaning the main part of the deck, do a test on decking that is hidden to check if your decking can withstand the pressure of the water. The water will literally gouge soft woods like cedar if the washer tip is brought too close to the surface. The same is true for the siding of your house or the skin on your foot, so wear protective clothing on your feet, hands, and face.

Once you have determined the proper distance to maintain between the tip of the washer and the deck, the fun can begin. Pressure washing is an immensely rewarding activity because the results are instantaneous.

Spray on a deck cleaner and allow it work for 10 minutes to 15 minutes.

Using a stiff-bristle brush, scrub the decking in the direction of the wood grain. Then rinse the surface with a pressure washer.

REPAIR WHAT THE WEATHER HAS WRECKED

When approaching repair, start with the most obvious problems. Look for deck boards that are starting to rot or are badly checked. For these boards, it is often easier to replace the entire board rather than just cut out the bad part. Think of replacing a board as doing surgery. You will need to take out the bad part while protecting everything else. If you have an extra sheet of plywood, lay that down to work off of and stage your tools. Reciprocating saws and multitools can be extremely useful for cutting fasteners that are fused to the wood (like galvanized nails) or weak from corrosion (like screw shanks).

Replacing other elements of the deck is an even greater challenge because, like the deck boards, you have to fight fasteners and make precision cuts without damaging the surrounding deck. In addition, surrounding pieces of the deck need temporary support so that they don't sag, fall, or rack during the repair. As always, take the time to think through all phases of your project so there

aren't any ugly surprises when the saw makes its way all through the piece of wood.

Finally, give the deck a once over and tighten any fasteners that worked loose during the seasons. The expansion and contraction of wood and other materials can work fasteners loose. To really be effective, look for loose fasteners at the driest time of the year when the wood has shrunk to its smallest dimensions.

In hardwood decking, **seasonal torque can pull screws up.**

PROTECT YOUR WORK WITH A FINISH COAT

The first year or two, no matter what type of finish you've chosen, you will want to apply a coat in the spring and fall. After that, the frequency of touching up the finish coat will depend on the look you want.

If you've let the deck go gray and are just using a sealant for protection, then one coat a year should be sufficient. If you've decided to try to maintain a new natural-wood appearance, then be prepared to get your brush out two or even three times a year.

The more pigment a finish has, the more it will act like paint. Like paint, this type of finish tends to peel if you aren't careful when applying it. The surface needs to be clean, dry, and undamaged by the sun.

If you're using more than one can of finish, **mix all the cans together for a uniform color.**

PROTECT YOUR WORK WITH A FINISH COAT (CONTINUED)

1 To prevent lap marks, spray on the finish one board at a time.

2 Use a painter's pad on a long pole to smooth out the layer of finish applied with the sprayer.

3 Allow the finish to be absorbed fully (about 10 minutes) and then remove the excess with a rag or a rag-covered scrub brush.

4 The refinished deck.

DECK MAINTENANCE CHECKLIST

Completing this simple checklist of maintenance items will remove much of the guesswork of what to do.

- **Clear it.** Keep the deck clear of debris. Don't use a deck as a storage area for lumber, yard supplies, tools, or other items that should be stored in a garden shed.

- **Clean it.** Have a regular cleaning schedule and stick to it. Most decks require cleaning only twice a year.

- **Protect it.** Regularly apply a sealer, stain, or paint. As with cleaning, establish a regular schedule and stick to it.

- **Inspect it.** While doing your regular maintenance, take the time to inspect the deck for rot, insects, and other damage.

- **Repair it.** You don't have to fix every issue as soon as you find it but be sure to make time to address problem areas during the time of regular maintenance. One small issue can become a major problem if left unattended.

- **Invest in it.** Continue to improve you deck and modify it to suit your changing needs. The more you use your deck, the more apt you are to take good care of it.

Use a brush for stairs and other tight spots **that are too awkward to spray. A handheld painting pad also works well for applying finish to areas too small to spray.**

WORKING ON AN EXISTING DECK

Deck rehab is the subject of its own book, but if the deck is in relatively good condition a quick run-through of important items will clarify a maintenance plan.

First, you'll want to look at the framing to make sure the deck is safe for your family and friends. If possible, get under the deck and inspect the ledger attachment. Make sure the ledger is not rotted and has adequate fasteners. It's all too common to find a ledger that's secured with only 16d nails. Reinforce the fasteners where necessary and replace any boards that are rotted. You can also reinforce other framing connections by adding framing hardware at key locations, such as where the joists connect to the ledger and where the posts support beams.

Second, look at the decking itself and repair or replace any decking that is rotted or severely checked. Look for areas of the deck that have suffered damage.

If one area of the deck has rot in both the framing and decking, then you may have a larger water-maintenance issue. Look to failing gutters and debris from trees for the main causes of excess water on your deck.

Third, address safety issues. Poorly attached guard railings are a common structural safety issue. To reinforce guardrails you will have to get underneath the deck and add hardware or extra blocking to the post attachment. For railings, also inspect the balusters, rails, and caps to ensure that they are correctly secured and free of rot.

Finally, with any deck, a fresh coat of sealant is a good idea. Once you've taken care of the glaring issues establish a schedule for regular cleaning, sealing, and repair (see "Deck Maintenance Checklist" on the facing page).

RESOURCES

BOOKS

Anderson, L. O., Heebink, T. B., and Oviatt, A. E. *Construction Guides for Exposed Wood Decks*. U.S. Forest Service, 1972. Some of the information is dated but much is still pertinent. Provides a good historical picture of best practices for deck construction just as the industry was building steam.

Mathewson, Glenn. *Deck Construction Based on the 2009 International Residential Code*. International Code Council, 2009. Expert guidance through the building code as it relates to deck construction.

Winterbottom, Daniel. *Wood in the Landscape: A Practical Guide to Specification and Design*. Wiley, 2000. Informative overview of the use of wood in the exterior environment.

WEBSITES

Fine Homebuilding magazine
www.finehomebuilding.com
Great resource not only for deck building but for all phases of residential construction.

North American Deck and Railing Association
www.nadra.org
Professional organization devoted to the deck-building industry; good resource for decking ideas and also a good place to start when looking for deck builders in your area.

Professional Deck Builder magazine
www.deckmagazine.com
Magazine devoted specifically to the deck-building industry.

www.wwpa.org
Trade association for western lumber manufacturers. Publishes good technical reports concerning various types of lumber.

www.awc.org
American Wood Council. Publishers of the DCA6, the prescriptive residential deck guide.

www.diamondpier.com
Pin foundation system that works well when excavation of footings is not a viable option.

www.calculated.com
Makers of a wide assortment of construction calculators that are invaluable when laying out stairs, cutting rafters, determining square footage, etc. They also now have an app for their calculators, which will work on most phones.

www.deckwedge.com
Deck Wedge Board Straightener

SUPPLIES

Bigfoot Systems
www.bigfootsystems.com
Pier footing forms

FastenMaster
www.fastenmaster.com
Not only has a great selection of screws for deck building but also offers good hidden fastener choices.

GRK Fasteners®
www.grkfasteners.com
Great selection of screws for all phases of deck construction

Hardwood Wrench™
www.hardwoodwrench.com
The best deck board straightening tool on the market

Kreg Tool Deck Jig
www.kregtool.com
Versatile deck-fastening system that hides the screws from sight.

Simpson Strong-Tie
www.strongtie.com
The leader in mechanical connectors for wood construction

Square Foot
www.sqfoot.com
Concrete footing forms

USP Structural Connectors
www.uspconnectors.com
Engineered structural connectors, anchors, and software solutions

INDEX

If you like this book, you'll love *Fine Homebuilding*.